ON THE TRAIL

THE LIFE AND TALES OF "LEAD STEER" POTTER

"Lead Steer" Potter

ON THE TRAIL

THE LIFE AND TALES OF "LEAD STEER" POTTER

By Jean M. Burroughs

Original Stories by Col. Jack Potter

MUSEUM OF NEW MEXICO PRESS
SANTA FE

CREDITS

"Lead Steers" was edited by S. Omar Barker for *Ranch Romances*, January 1948.

"Case Closed" was edited by S. Omar Barker for *Ranch Romances*, October 1940.

"Pot Hook Johnson" was edited by S. Omar Barker for *Ranch Romances*, July 1947.

"The Jingle-Bob Herd" was edited by George Fitzpatrick for *New Mexico Magazine*, July 1945.

"Dragging a Big Loop" was edited by George Fitzpatrick for *New Mexico Magazine*, July 1935; reprinted in *Union County Leader*, July 4, 1935.

"Roundup Court" was edited by George Fitzpatrick for *New Mexico Magazine*, September 1946.

"That Orneriest Steer" was edited by Belle Kilgore, WPA Writers' Project (WPA Writers' Project Files, 1937, State Records Center and Archives, Santa Fe, New Mexico). This story appeared with the title "Buckshot Roberts" in Jack Potter's *Cattle Trails of the Old West*.

"Killing the Lobo Wolf" is from WPA Writers' Project (WPA Writers' Project Files, 1937, State Records Center and Archives, Santa Fe, New Mexico). Also in *Union County Leader*, undated clipping in Potter Files.

"The Sanctified Texan" appeared in the *Union County Leader*, September 15, 1932.

"The Indian Scare" is an unpublished manuscript in Potter Files.

"Tragedies on the Portales Road" was rewritten by Jean M. Burroughs from an original story in the *Union County Leader*, undated clipping in Potter Files.

"Early-Day Saloons" is from the *Union County Leader*, undated clipping in Potter Files.

"The Old Bunk House" is from the *Union County Leader*, undated clipping in Potter Files.

"A Delayed Christmas" is from the *Union County Leader*, undated clipping in Potter Files.

"The Battle of Estancia Grant" is from the *Union County Leader*, undated clipping in Potter Files.

"Negro Cowboys" is from the *Union County Leader*, undated clipping in Potter Files.

"Death and Burial of Billy the Kid" appeared as an account by Jack Potter in the *Union County Leader*, undated clipping in Potter Files.

"Cowboy and Sheep Governors" was published as "Cowboy and Sheep Governors," *Santa Fe New Mexican*, and as "Cattlemen in Governor's Mansion," *Union County Leader*, both on April 4, 1932.

Library of Congress Catalog Number: 79-93061
ISBN 089013-131-7 (hard cover)

Museum of New Mexico Press
P.O. Box 2087
Santa Fe, New Mexico 87503

FOREWORD

W hat a joy to visit again with Col. Jack Potter in the pages of *On the Trail*. What a fund of stories he had about the pioneer days. What a robust sense of humor!

Reading about him after all these years makes him seem as alive and vigorous and as cheerful and amusing as in the nearly twenty years I knew him before his death in 1950.

In my early newspaper years we carried on a continuing correspondence as he commented on items in the "Off the Beaten Path" column I was writing for the *Albuquerque Tribune*. Sometimes items would trigger a recollection of his own younger days, and he would write of people, events, often wild and woolly yarns of early cowboying and trail driving. His letters made good copy.

I did not meet him in person until 1935 when I went to Santa Fe as editor of *New Mexico Magazine*. One of the first stories I bought was his "Trail Dust," a story about a steer named Lew Wallace, which appeared in the February 1935 issue. And there were more of Jack Potter's yarns in the months and years that followed.

In that first year of our acquaintance I asked him how he got the title of Colonel, thinking that he might have been in the military. He kind of hemmed and hawed about it and finally gave me the impression it had just kind of grew on him with age. I thought it ought to be made official, and I asked Governor Clyde Tingley to appoint him an honorary colonel on his staff. A letter from Col. Jack on September 23, 1935 tells the result: "I have received your letter of recent date, also my commission appointment as Colonel. Tell the Governor that nothing could have pleased me better, and I thank him for the honor."

Col. Jack was representing Union County in the Legislature in those days, and he would always come to the magazine office for a visit when he was in Santa Fe. At the 1940 session, he did not show up. But about the middle of January I got a note from him.

"I expect you have wondered what has become of me," he wrote. "Only a few days after arriving here I was sent to San Vincent hospital with an infected toe, was there ten days, and before turning the old Lead Steer loose, his diet was changed from Black Grama and snow water to that of sagebrush and polluted stale water. And was throwed into a Jersey cut-back bunch. I don't give a darn, I'm still the old lead steer, and I'm going to run with the lead cattle, *sabe?*"

As Jean Burroughs has mentioned, Frank King, trail driver and historian, called Col. Jack "the most cheerful liar west of the Mississippi." Commenting on this, Col. Jack wrote me that "Should I ever make the grade as being the most cheerful liar in the state, I will have to give you credit for the achievement." The reason for the comment was that I was always discouraging Col. Jack about his wanting to write historical fact articles. I urged him to stick with his own experiences and reminiscences. He responded, "I have never been able to interest you in historical fact stories, but am glad you like my stories of my experiences. I know that it would kill a cowboy plumb dead to tell his experiences without handling the truth in a hazardous way."

Col. Jack wrote five articles for *New Mexico Magazine* in 1935, then an occasional one over the years until 1949 when his last one appeared in the April 1949 edition. But at age eighty-six he was still writing an occasional letter. The last one he wrote me in 1950 a few months before he died was a long discussion "correcting some errors of big writers," as he put it, concerning Billy the Kid.

When he died in November 1950 he was among the last of those wonderfully colorful old characters who had lived through the violent days of the 1880s and 90s when Eastern New Mexico was open range for thousands of cattle. Fortunately he had the gift of storytelling, and he has left us a rich heritage of material to enjoy and appreciate. He was indeed "the lead steer" of a herd of writers on the days of the open range.

George Fitzpatrick
Albuquerque, New Mexico
January, 1980

ACKNOWLEDGEMENTS

This book is Jack Potter's own life story, told essentially through his writings, which were begun in later years after his trail and ranching days were over. To facts of his biography I have added research on a few major topics which loomed large in his varied career. Chief of these areas were the Potter–Bacon cutoff trail, blazed by Jack Potter himself; the New England Cattle Company, whose four large ranches figured so prominently in his life; his service to the New Mexico legislature; his membership in several Trail Drivers organizations; and his long tenure as a "Marrying Justice" of the Peace of Union County.

I am indebted to his daughter, Mrs. Ethel Potter Wade of Clayton, New Mexico, now deceased; to his son, R.E. Potter, age ninety-four years, who resides in Albuquerque; and to Cordelia Lenhart Burleigh of Lubbock, a granddaughter, for family clippings, scrapbooks, and personal accounts. The Special Collections of Eastern New Mexico University Library under the direction of Mrs. Mary Jo Walker, Archivist, generously allowed me to use the Potter papers and manuscripts donated to that institution. I am especially grateful to D.H. Haley, former principal of the Clayton schools, who gave a personal insight into the character and reputation of his fellow townsman.

S. Omar Barker of Las Vegas, New Mexico graciously granted permission to include in my text his humorous poem, "Jack Potter's Courtin'," as well as three Potter stories, edited by Barker, which were published in *Ranch Romances*. George Fitzpatrick, former editor of *New Mexico Magazine*, allowed me to use stories that he edited and published and for which I give special thanks. The editors of *The Cattleman*, *New Mexico Stockman*, and the *Union County Leader* have all permitted me to use the published Potter stories on which there is no copyright. For purposes of this book I have condensed and re-edited them.

Dr. Myra Ellen Jenkins, New Mexico State Historian, State Records Center, Santa Fe, was of great assistance to me in research on the Fort Sumner headquarters and land holdings, and in addition furnished me copies of Potter stories from the WPA Writers' Project, namely "The Indian Scare," "Killing the Lobo Wolf," and "That Orneriest Steer," which were told by Jack Potter to writers in that program. Her personal interest was greatly appreciated.

I am grateful to Mrs. Myrtle Stedman of Santa Fe, who furnished drawings by her late husband, Wilfred Stedman, that had previously illustrated Potter's stories in the *New Mexico Magazine*. Line drawings by Wilfred Stedman and H. D. Bugbee are to be found in the Potter files, special collections, Eastern New Mexico University Library, Portales.

J. Evetts Haley of Canyon, Texas, who allowed me to review his correspondence with Jack Potter, and his secretary Mrs. Velma Larsen, who graciously provided assistance during my work in the Haley office, were especially helpful.

Mrs. Horace Bailey Carroll of Austin, Texas permitted the use of Dr. Carroll's letter to Jack Potter concerning the route of the Fort Smith–Santa Fe Trail.

The Dobie Collection, Humanities Research Center, University of Texas permitted me to quote excerpts from Potter letters to J. Frank Dobie and to use photos of those letters.

Jean M. Burroughs
Portales, New Mexico
September, 1979

CONTENTS

THE LIFE OF
COL. JACK POTTER

ONE

FIGHTIN'
PARSON'S BOY

"Where can I find this fellow, Lead Steer Potter?" asked a stranger who had stopped briefly in the little cow town of Clayton, New Mexico.

"You mean Colonel Jack?" the clerk at R.W. Isaacs Hardware questioned as he wrapped up a box of hunting shells. He pointed across the street to the Eklund Hotel, where a few old-timers sat on sidewalk benches, swapping stories. Warm sunshine cast a mellow glow on the tan sandstone walls and deepened the creases in their weatherworn faces. A big man in a tall Stetson hat rose, slapped a few friends on the back in a genial goodbye gesture, and started away from the group.

"That's him, coming this way now," exclaimed the clerk. "He's an old trail driver who spins some mighty fancy yarns about the good old cow-days. He'll talk on and on if you just get him started. That's not hard to do, either."

The newcomer making the purchases watched Jack Potter cross the street, cheerily waving a huge hand to passersby. As he came closer, the clerk called to him, "Come over, Colonel Jack, there's somebody here who wants to talk to you."

Erect and moving easily with a long stride, Potter cut across to the hardware store. His Stetson revealed a shock of greying hair under the

3

sweat-stained brim. His old coat, casually unbuttoned, showed a striped shirt and elastic suspenders with no belt to confine his huge girth.

The clerk introduced the stranger to Potter and added, "He says that his Pa knew your Pa back in the circuit riding days of south Texas."

The man extended his hand. "Glad to know you, sir. My Pa has often told me about your Pa, the Fightin' Parson."

Potter's eyes twinkled. "Yep, that's what they called him, all right. He carried a gun along with his Bible, often right into the pulpit. Yes, I'm known as the Fightin' Parson's boy. Come home with me and I'll ask the missus to make us coffee while we talk about our past."

When they were seated on his wide front porch, Potter began to reminisce. "Pa told us children many stories about his younger days—when he was at home long enough to sit a spell. Our Ma mostly raised us, thirteen living children and two dead. She didn't have much to go on either, just what folks could spare when the collection plate was passed at camp meetings and circuit church gatherings.

"My Pa was named Andrew Jackson Potter, after Old Hickory of Tennessee. He was orphaned when he was only ten years old and drifted into Missouri in 1832 with some traders who taught him how to ride, shoot, and play cards. He joined as a teamster in 1846 with General Sterling Price when he followed the Santa Fe Trail into New Mexico. Pa worked in copper mines in Arizona and finally drifted back to Texas. He married my mother, Emily Guin, in 1852 and freighted lumber from Bastrop to San Marcos. Fifteen dollars a month was big pay in those days for that kind of work, but it was a real rough life. He told us later that he sure held his own among all those drunkards and gamblers.

"Somehow, he and his partner, a feller named Smithwick, got converted in a revival at Croft's Prairie, Texas. My Pa was never a man to do anything half way, and pretty soon he was preaching himself. About 1859 he sold out in Bastrop County and moved to Caldwell County, nine miles east of Lockhart, where he got himself a license to preach and ride circuit. He had a booming voice and deep blue eyes that seemed to shoot sparks at those sinners. He said he got their attention all right and they listened to his preaching and praying." Jack Potter chuckled appreciatively at the memory of his Pa.

"When the Civil War broke out, since he was not in the regular ministerial ranks, he was subject to Confederate conscription law. He preferred to volunteer, and during the latter part of the Civil War he became chaplain for De Bray's Regiment of Texas cavalry. It was about this time he picked up the name of 'Fightin' Parson.' He used to tell us children of how he'd mingle with his men, reading from his Bible, praying for their safety in battle. Then when the bugle blew to charge, how he'd pocket the Good

Book, grab his musket, and lead in the fight to 'usher them Yankees into the promised land.'

"About the end of the Civil War on December 11, 1864, I was born at Prairielee, Texas and named Jack Myers after Pa's commanding colonel just as he had been named for his Pa's superior officer. We lived there until we moved to San Antonio in 1869. I recall that journey very well, for some of us children rode in the *cuna* or stretched cowhide hung underneath the wagon like a hammock. It sure was dusty. The dogs trotted along beside us and sometimes we would be rocked to sleep by the swaying of the old cuna as the wagon creaked along.

"We located on the stage line between San Antonio and El Paso, near what was later the Western Cattle Trail. Pa would preach to the passengers when they laid over at our house for a rest. He was good natured and friendly, most of the time—that is, except when his boys gave him a peck of trouble.

"Pa treasured his old Winchester which a friend gave him and kept it beside him always, in the saddle or buggy, and even propped up against the pulpit, if there was one. He preached to sinners in saloons just as regular as to cowboys on the range as he made his rounds. Sometimes he arrived just in time to conduct funeral services and give a decent burial to some feller who had gone on to meet his Maker. Sometimes he read wedding ceremonies too and comforted the sick.

"One of his first assignments was as a Methodist minister in Kerrville, Texas in 1867. Later he served in Bandera, Coleman, and Tom Green counties as well as Mason clear down to Uvalde County. He established the first church in San Angelo in 1880. Some of the gamblers in saloons there, converted or still sinners, got up enough money for him to use in building what was later was known as the Methodist Church. He was a staunch believer and was diligent in his crusade for the Lord. His circuits took him such distances on horseback that he did not return home for months at a time. My Ma never complained much about this. It seemed a way of life for most women, I guess.

"I recollect how he told us boys about the time when his ponies were staked out for the night in the rough brush country and some thief crept up to loose the hobbles and drive them off. My Pa and a boy who was traveling with him were resting on the ground just before dawn. Pa had taken off his shoes and pants, as the weather was quite hot. When he heard them ponies stampin' and whinnyin' he grabbed his shoes, his gun, but didn't have time to pull on his pants. He chased the thief through the thorny brush until he lost sight of him and had to give up the pursuit because his legs up to his thighs were so filled with thorns and stickers that he could hardly walk. The boy helped him pull out the biggest thorns, but Pa had to endure the stinging burn of the smallest ones until he could ride into San Felipe and find a pair of tweezers." Potter slapped his knee and laughed heartily. "We always found this particular story highly entertaining, as us boys could hardly imagine our preacher Pa running through the brush minus his pants!" Then Potter turned to his guest and asked, "Where's your Pa? When did he know the Fightin' Parson?"

The man instantly stifled his chuckle and became somber and reflective. "I've heard my Pa tell it many a time, Colonel Potter, that he was in the congregation there in Tilmon Chapel in 1895 when the Fightin' Parson was winding up a powerful sermon on the text 'What Think Ye of Christ?' His voice had been booming out exhortations to the sinners to repent when he suddenly spoke in hushed tones, so faint that only those on the front row could hear. 'I think you have just heard my last preachin'; I'm goin' home to meet my . . .' Then he fell forward from the pulpit, limp and lifeless."

The two men sat silent a moment, each with his own thoughts and memories. The visitor rose, shook Potter's hand. "I'm pleased to meet you, sir. I promised my Pa I would look you up if ever I was near where you lived. You see, my Pa was converted that very day during that last sermon. He told me he would never forget that service. Well, I'd best be going."

Jack Potter nodded his head and shook hands with his visitor as he turned to leave and head back to where his car was parked. "I must go in and tell my missus about this," he said, half to himself. "She'll be real glad to know."

*   *   *

Like his father, Jack had been on his own, beginning at an early age. As a young boy he had watched the trail herds move past his home on the old stagecoach road and promised himself that he too would follow the trail, if not as a preacher or stage driver, then as a cowhand who lived a free and adventurous life. "One of my exciting experiences," he later recalled, "was the ride into town on top of the daily stagecoach that rumbled past our house. My brothers and I would wait for the stage as it came around a bend in the road, a-rockin' and a-swayin'. Pop Howard, the owner, was sure a favorite with us, because he had the driver slow down long enough for us boys to clamber up and ride into town, a-whoopin' and a-hollerin'. There were frequent reports of Indian raids and robberies, but that didn't dim our ambition to become stage drivers ourselves."

Jack Potter was strongly built with a heavy frame, standing nearly his mature height of six foot four by the time he was fourteen. His broad grin and easygoing good humor made him a favorite among the rough drovers with whom he worked as a brush hand, beginning when he was twelve years old. He had hunted rabbits as a youngster in the brush country of south Texas, so it was no hardship now to him to push through the overhanging trees and undergrowth to herd the wayward cattle and point them on the trail. He was proud to be a "brush popper."

"In 1876," Potter recounted later, "my wages were a dollar a day, following the herds through the brush at all seasons of the year. When I was sixteen, I hired on as a driver, mite young, but they were short-handed and took a chance on me when I bragged that I had been a brush hand for the past four years.

"I was supposed to be let off after we had gone part way, when all the other extra hands turned back. But the daylight to dark hours, poorly cooked grub, and constant exposure to bad weather was too much for me and I took chills and fever. The boss sent me back when we reached Granite Mountain. We stopped for a while so that all the lame cattle could be cut out and left with the trail cutter. I heard Jess Tiner, the boss, tell Jim Speer, who was in charge of the camp, 'I don't have much to drop off with you this time, just one lame yearling and one sick kid.' I sure hated to be classed in with a lame yearling.

"Jim was a hard-boiled old cuss and acted like he didn't want to be burdened with me, but he finally took pity on my shaking and chilling and gave me two tablespoons full of cayenne pepper, telling me to repeat the dose every time I felt a chill coming on. Believe me, that was the last chill I had, and in two days time I left old Dr. Speer and hit the trail back home."

A child became a boy, expected to shoulder responsibility, by the time he was twelve, and a man by age fifteen or sixteen. So it was with Jack Potter. He rode hard, learning the ways of cattle as well as of men. One of Jack's greatest satisfactions was to hunker down close to the campfire after a day of strenuous exertion. Here he listened to hair-raising exaggerations of Indian raids and cattle stampedes, and here too he learned the lingo of cowmen, how to spin a few "windies" himself, and how to bear up under the brunt of raw jokes.

He learned to tell time and direction by the stars at night; to observe how a prevailing wind bent grass and drifted sand into rippling patterns; to watch the behavior of cattle as they neared water; and, above all, to know the signs of quick restlessness that would cause a stampede. He learned to keep the cows milling in a circle to prevent their running, and to chant old cowboy songs in a singsong deep rumble to quiet them on the bed-ground.

Potter's first trip as a trail hand was in 1882, when he signed on with the New England Livestock Company to help drive 3,000 head from southwest Texas to Cheyenne, Wyoming. After that, he was no longer a green kid but a man to be trusted and depended upon. The Fightin' Parson's boy had grown up.[1]

TWO

TRAILING UP
FROM SOUTH TEXAS

The trail drive of 1882 came at the height of cattle herding to northern markets. Trailing began as early as 1886, when Charles Goodnight went from San Angelo, Texas to the lush grasslands of eastern Colorado and north to Cheyenne. It was the start of the West's development. John Chisum followed this same trail from his ranch on the Concho River in Tom Green County, Texas along the Pecos River to Fort Sumner, New Mexico, where for about two years he sold his cattle to the Government Indian Agency.

Even earlier, in Oklahoma and Kansas, a half-breed Cherokee named Jesse Chisholm (last name pronounced the same but spelled differently from that of the Texas rancher), broke a number of trails with his trading wagons. Later, in 1865 on government contract, he moved Indians from around Wichita, Kansas to Anadarko, Oklahoma on the Washita River.[1] Jesse Chisholm was not a cattleman or herder, and contrary to later misconceptions about his route, he never traded as far south as Texas. His trail from Wichita to Indian Territory was the true Chisholm Trail that is often mentioned in stories of the early West.

Writers who romanticized cowboys on the trail in the 1880s generally failed to mention the fact that the first cattle trailing began in 1540, when

Coronado's entourage brought vast numbers of stringy cattle up from Mexico. For many years afterward, New Mexico was the destination of cattle driven north to supply the chain of missions established under Spanish rule in the 1700s. Vaqueros were not only the first cattlemen and cowboys, but the first trail drivers as well.[2]

The lush grass and mild climate of south Texas caused the Spanish cattle to increase enormously, and as a consequence, cowmen were forced to seek markets elsewhere. In 1836, when settlers from the east came to colonize the new Republic of Texas, cattle were driven both north and east until buyers could be found. Farther on to Arkansas, Kansas, Nebraska, and Ohio, the Texas cattle were herded in long dusty lines, beginning in 1852. The first *reported* Texas herd came to St. Louis in 1854.[3]

The Texas cattle industry had begun to develop before Jack Potter was born, as the vast unsettled lands in the West provided ample breeding and grazing grounds. It did not take much capital in those days—the initiative to find a suitable range with water holes and the courage to defend his stake were the chief requirements for a successful cattleman. Gun fighters were hired right along with cowboys in most outfits.

In the year of Potter's birth, 1864, the Civil War had caused a crisis in the cattle industry of south Texas. Men had been taken away from their homes to fight with the Confederates and their herds had been neglected. When they returned, the lack of markets for the large natural increase drove the price down to as low as one to five dollars a head. Beef in the northern markets still commanded a good price, but reaching those markets through hostile Indian territory and difficult terrain, with rivers to ford and mountains to cross, made cattle trailing a hazardous and often tragic business. Nevertheless, Texas cowmen were willing to take those chances.

Cattle began to move north in tremendous numbers as soon as the Kansas Pacific Railroad built westward from Kansas City in 1867. Now cattlemen could ship herds to market in the north, if they could successfully drive them to the shipping points which were established along extended rail lines.[4]

The bosses of those first drives were the ranchers themselves or their more experienced cowboys. Their crews were often made up of ex-soldiers newly discharged from military duties, former freighters out of a trade route, and the usual ne'er-do-wells and petty criminals who were looking for adventure and an escape from justice.[5]

The cattle moving north from south Texas at this time usually went by the Eastern Trail, which started at several different points in the coastal ranges, mainly those of the King Ranch in Nueces County up to Gonzales, Waco, and Fort Worth, to Nocono on the Red River. In this area it joined the Jesse Chisholm trade route, which crossed the whole of Indian Territory to reach markets in Abilene, Kansas.

Lanky and tall for his age, Jack Potter was almost old enough to serve as a brush popper when the Western Trail, blazed by D.S. Combs, began to move by his home on the Overland Stage route.[6] "My Pa," he wrote in his reminiscences, "was selected by the Sheriff of Kendall County to escort the trail drivers through our county as others did in Bexar and Kerr Counties. This escorting of herds amounted to blazing a new trail, branching off as it did from the Eastern which went by Austin, Fort Worth on north to cross Red River. It was really the beginning of the Western Trail and the year was 1876."[7]

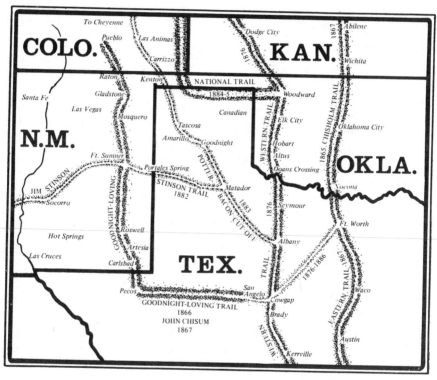

Major Western cattle trails, including the Potter-Bacon Cutoff.

The Western Trail also started in extreme south Texas. It went by San Antonio, Kerrville, and Coleman, up to Albany in central Texas, then crossed at Doan's Store on the Red River near present-day Vernon. It also went up through Indian Territory but to the west of the Chisholm Trail, reaching Woodward, Oklahoma and then veering northwest to Dodge. There drovers replenished supplies before pushing northward on an extension of the Western Trail called the Northern which went north by Ogallala, Pine Bluff, Chugwater, and Powder River to the Black Hills.

On Potter's first trail ride in 1882, when he was eighteen, some 3,000 head were to be brought from south Texas by the New England Livestock

Company. There were four bosses to handle this trip, the herd being divided among them in fairly equal bunches. King Hannant of Corpus Christi was boss of the first herd; Asa Clark of Lagarta was in charge of the second; Billie Burk handled the third; while John Smith of San Antonio was responsible for the fourth, the one in which Jack Potter rode with old lead steer Randau pointing the way.[8]

The herders were pushed to find sufficient grass and water for such a large number of animals, and in their wanderings they missed the river crossing at the intended spot on the Canadian, drifting farther down to Tascosa, the toughest cow town young Jack had ever seen. He had been forced by the cook's illness to drive the chuck wagon with a four mule team. The noise and confusion in the little settlement so upset his mules they nearly got out of hand and ran away, but Jack's physical strength and experience in handling the reins saved the wagon from turning turtle and scattering its pots, beans, and bacon over the prairie. It caused him great chagrin, however, when he found his gun had been tossed out in the mad dash. Jack complained to his boss after the team had quieted down that the old fightin' cusses had cost him his weapon and left him defenseless for a spell. A man without his gun was in as bad shape in those days as a man without his pants.

In Tascosa Jack was initiated into the excitement and bawdy entertainment of saloon and dance hall. A run on merchants' stocks, particularly the liquid kind, when cowboys swarmed into the little town brought needed cash into Tascosa coffers. Several big cattle outfits, the LIT and LX and others in that section of the country, had converged on Tascosa in the summer of 1882. News of the roundup had drawn camp followers, gamblers, and drifters. Emigrant caravan wagons as well as thousands of herd cattle stirred up the dust of this rowdy settlement on the Canadian River.

Not only Jack's mules but his company's entire herd was agitated by the unaccustomed confusion and racket. Left and right point riders had a difficult time keeping their animals from breaking out over the range as they left the old town behind them. Only after crossing the Canadian did the old "high-hipped" lead steer finally strike a steady pace. The lowing protests of the cattle diminished as they moved on to Trinidad, Colorado through the mountain pass of northern New Mexico.

Here the four herds were combined into two large bunches, as the trail would now be easier with abundant grass and water. All extra hands were to be laid off at Trinidad, Jack Potter included. That wily young cowhand was determined to go on to Greeley, however, and he disappeared from the camp, remaining away until he was sure that all discharged hands had headed back for Texas. Then he came riding back one morning with a newborn calf that needed attention slung across his saddle.

"You had orders to leave the trail at Trinidad," John Smith growled at him, ignoring the piteous "moo" of the calf.

Big Jack just stood there grinning, hat in hand, as he stroked the calf's smooth coat. "I'll put this critter in the calf wagon; maybe I can find a rancher along the way who can care for her," he offered.

"Go ahead, one extra tenderfoot won't hurt nothin'," said his manager. "But don't try that stunt again, at least no ways soon."

Ashamed to reveal his feeling of relief, the kindhearted boy hurried to stow the puny calf in the wagon, safe with others that were unable to walk the trail—but he gave it an extra pat for saving his job for the trip farther north.[9]

Then Jack rode back to his position as flank or swing driver, one which was just ahead of the drags. His job was to keep the herd moving together in orderly fashion. He helped to pace the drags or slower cattle and prevent their slowing down too much. He was lucky not to be demoted to riding left drag. That was the worst position in the trail, for the constantly drifting dust was well nigh intolerable. Draggers usually rode with neckerchiefs over their faces like a bunch of bandits, their hats pulled low and eyes squinted.

Finally, when the trail-hardy crew reached Greeley, the lead steer and his plodding herd were turned out to graze the luxuriant upland grass and mature for market. It cost about $1 a head to move a cow up from Texas to Montana. On this drive, costs totaled about $3,000. Even though herders expected to lose about three percent of their cattle on a long drive, they still realized a profit of about $3 to $4 a head in those days.[10] Cowhands earned an average of $30 a month while a trail boss drew $100. Jack promised himself that he would be a boss—not sooner or later, but sooner.

Northern ranches such as the New England Livestock Company spread were much better equipped to care for the trail hands than the camps in the warmer climates of south Texas. In Greeley the boys who were going north with a herd of 150 cow ponies were outfitted with cots, warmer bedding, and a big wall-sided tent. Especially to the cowboys' liking, however, was the bigger chuck wagon with better grub served by trained cooks.[11]

Jack signed up to go with them, and after leaving Cheyenne he started out for Powder River and Sheridan, Wyoming. As the weather got colder he got more homesick, and he was not sorry upon reaching the Crow Indian Agency to find a letter directing him to leave immediately for Texas where he would be needed to help prepare for the spring drive. In later years Jack recounted many times his first train trip and first overnight stay in a hotel, probably adding a few descriptive details with each telling. The eighteen-year-old greenhorn told it this way.

"One morning the trail boss paid me off and gave me a ticket to Denver on the Union Pacific. 'I had a heap rather ride my horse back,' I told him. 'I can make it to San Antonio in about forty days.'

"Well, he wouldn't listen to me, said it was the New England's policy to sell the horse and ship the man back by train. I tied my wage check and loose change into the corner of my shirttail and loaded up my saddle and camp equipment in a tin trunk tied up with about 200 feet of rope.

"I'd rather try to stop a stampede than to ride that bucking iron horse. The rattling rails and screeching whistle sure bothered me. Finally I settled down to enjoy the scenery and duck the bridge posts that came flying at me everytime we crossed a creek. The conductor came by and took my ticket away from me. All he gave me in return was a little red stub which he stuck in my hatband. Now that worried me, for the stub didn't have San Antonio written on it. I sure didn't think I would ever get back to Texas.

"As soon as I started down the aisle after him to show him his mistake, the swaying of the cars over the rough roadbed and my high heeled boots, slippin' on them hard slick floors, threw me right against the seat opposite me. I plumb near upset a woman carrying a little boy to the wash room.

"When I got to Denver, I looked up the St. Charles Hotel, went to a barber shop, and got a shave and haircut, but I sure was surprised when the barber suggested that I might want a bath. After nearly hog-scaldin' myself in a tub filled with hot water, slippin' on the marble floor and purt nigh crackin' my ribs, I set out to take in the town. At the Tabor Opera House I saw the first real live playacting I had ever witnessed. Midnight found me still bummin' around, but shortly I went back to the hotel to turn in.

"The gaslight in a fancy brass holder on the wall wouldn't blow out very easy though. I took my Stetson and gave it a good fanning but it still stayed lit. I gave up as I was too tired to stay awake all night trying to put out that light. Just put my hat over my eyes and slept till dawn when I woke up to see that gol-durned light still a-flickerin'.

"I dressed real quick like and went to the station to see if my trunk was still there. The agent was nice to me and said the rail company paid men to look after baggage and that I wasn't needed to haul my trunk myself. Now that was real comfortin', and I walked around some to see the sights of Denver. Waitin' on trains was sure boring. I'd a heap rather been riding my pony toward Texas. At this rate I would have gotten there at about the same time, since I didn't get to Dodge until midnight and then had a twenty-four hour lay over. Twenty-four hours in Dodge to a young man of eighteen was no hardship, however. I met up with some Texas boys and took in every saloon and gambling joint in town. George Saunders, Jesse Pressnall, and Slim Johnson were there too. There were several purty good fist fights, but no killing that night.

"Some more old Texas boys with "Dog Face" Smith in the lead rode the train with me the next day. We pulled off onto a siding to wait for another train to pass and clear the tracks. Well, one engineer tooted his whistle real loud as his train roared by and purty nigh caused a stampede right in the railway car. The conductor threatened to put us all in the stock car unlessen we calmed down.

"After breakfast in Hutchinson, a layover in Emporia, we finally boarded the Missouri, Kansas, and Texas for Parsons, on through Indian Territory to Denison, Texas. We had to change cars again at Taylor, then boarded the International and Great Northern for San Antonio. More than four days' travel on as many railroads finally brought me to my journey's end, where I picked up a horse and rode south to the ranch."[12]

The spring of 1883 found Jack Potter again ready to hit the trail. The New England Company had received cattle at the Pena station located on the Texas and Mexican branch railway. He detoured around the heavy brush country, hit the San Antonio trail at Agua Dulce, and thence headed north by way of the Western Trail. That spring, drought had parched the land and salted the flats with alkali dust. "We trailed over seven hundred miles before we saw rain, and then it came—a gully washer. The wet clothing of the men and dripping coats of the herd attracted lightning that played along the horns of the animals and spurs and bridle bits of the riders. It was the worst storm I ever remember," recollected Potter to his pals at the end of the drive four months later.

"Soon after, I was sent back to Texas and arrived at Albany near Fort Griffin to fit out for a forty days' drive. Here I was given instructions from Alfred T. Bacon, manager of the New England Company, with a map which he figgered would save me about twenty days' time, if I could break out the trail that way. It was a barren trail that crossed the Llano Estacado —a trail of arid sameness that promised nothing better until we neared the Goodnight Ranch. After we reached Charlie "Bueno Noches' " spread, we hit Tascosa, Buffalo Springs, the Ox Ranch on the Cimarron, Fort Lyons on the Arkansas, thence to the South Platte River at the mouth of the Bijou. Later this same trail, sometimes called by different names, was traced on maps, but since I was the first one to follow Bacon's drawing, I was the one to blaze this trail which became known as the Potter–Bacon cutoff.

"I got through all right, but not before I had a run-in with the Goodnight people. I was forced to detour around their range on account of their cattle not being immune to tick fever, which had begun to plague all the southern herds. Leigh Dwyer, Goodnight's brother-in-law, informed me that this herd which I was driving was the first one which had ventured through from the Western Trail, and since I had blazed it, others would surely follow and give them a heap of trouble."[13]

15

As early as 1880, before Jack Potter ever trailed a cow, increased cattle deaths due to the passage of "ticky" south Texas herds forced a group of cowmen, under leadership of Charles Goodnight, to meet at Mobeeti for legal action on closing the trail through their ranges. Their purpose was to confine the herds to designated "lines of drive," with the old Rath buffalo trail as one and a more westerly trail by way of Blanco Canyon, the Tule, and Palo Duro Canyon headwater route up to Tascosa as another. This route bypassed their land.

"They dedicated a mile and a half of range on either side of the trails for the benefit of the drovers trying to keep cattle within bounds," Potter later wrote. "Goodnight built a large tank on Running Water Draw near the site of Plainview to furnish them with water. James Parks was sent with a chuck wagon and a common sod plow to mark the course of the trail."[14]

Officially organized in January 1881, the Panhandle Stock Association set out its goals and prepared itself to arbitrarily defend them. The members agreed that unless the state of Texas would sell land directly to them, at least a leasing program should be inaugurated for their protection. The south Texas free-grass people killed this proposal; they were more numerous and influential than the pioneering cattlemen of the northwestern Panhandle.

Usually herders could be persuaded to take the detours, but if they refused, they were held out by force until frost had killed the grass which harbored the contagious ticks dropped by south Texas cows. The Association staked inspectors out as far as the Spur country near the beginning of the alternate route. "If the trail bosses refused to turn back, the inspectors sent for help from the nearest ranches. With an injunction from Mobeeti, they held the herd off by armed force. This was the *Winchester Quarantine*."[15]

Jack Potter had certain prior knowledge of that quarantine and made a wise decision to go around. Later, when he delivered the herd without further incident to the Crow Creek Ranch, he told his boss, "I was forced to detour and give in to them steel barrels pointin' in my direction. There warn't much else I could do."

After this drive he rode the rails a second time to Dodge where he obtained his cowboy ticket at reduced rates back to San Antonio, but not before he had outfitted himself with a fine suit of clothes from the Wright–Beverly Company owned by his friend Bob Wright.

Jack made his way back to Corpus Christi to pick up another herd for the drive of 1884, which was headed by a steer called Bob Wright for his friend the storekeeper. The drought had limited grass and water to such an extent that this herd had to be trailed only one hundred miles to Victoria, then shipped as far as Colbert, Indian Territory, where they were unloaded and trailed from Dodge City to Cheyenne. The coming of rail lines and the beginning of a widespread influx of homesteaders and ranchers made trailing for hundreds of miles impossible and impractical. The years 1884 to 1888 were the last when dark rivers of longhorns flowed up from deep south Texas, but of course shorter trails to railheads continued to be followed, bringing cattle to northern markets.

O N   T H E   T R A I L
T O   R O M A N C E

In between trail drives, Potter continued as a hand with the New England Livestock Company in Texas. During the month of May, 1883, just after he had returned from a cattle roundup, he went to a cowboy picnic at Boerne near San Antonio. Of course girls of the community were invited even though many of the old boys were tongue-tied and embarrassed in feminine company. Not so Jack Potter, who immediately selected the prettiest gal of the bunch and asked to meet her.

Her name was Cordelia Peace Eddy and she came from Louisville, Kentucky, though she had been born in Texas. Many years later, when he began to write his memories of the old trailing days, he told this story of meeting his future wife. " 'Who is that young filly with the beautiful curls spilling out over her sunbonnet?' I asked a cowboy standing near me. 'Take me to her, I simply must meet her.'

"My friend cautioned me just to mill around in the crowd and let her get used to this rough bunch of fellows before I approached personally. 'Don't you remember about Helotes Bill being sent down to San Antone to meet a school teacher arriving from the East, and when Old Bill introduced himself, she became frightened and fell over in a dead faint?' one of the boys asked me.

"Yes, I sure remembered, but Old Helotes had a long moustache and a terrible personality. You couldn't blame that poor woman. It turned out that I got acquainted with this curly-headed gal, and for the next twelve months whenever I could get off, I would come in to see her. In a little while we began to write frequent letters.

"In the spring of 1884, I was receiving cattle and shaping up the herd for the next drive. While counting and checking out herd number one, I lost count of the critters three times, and the Texas manager of our company, who turned out to be an old matchmaker, said to me, 'Jack, you just as well own up, when a man can't count cattle, it's a cinch he's in love with some girl. I'll tell you what to do. It will be ten days before the second herd is ready. I'll give you a vacation so you can go home and propose to that sweetheart. You're too young to know how to use the proper diplomacy, but don't handle her like you're making a horse trade. If necessary, get down on your knees, weep, threaten to commit suicide. Keep staying with the situation until she says "yes." I know just how you feel, and even though you are the best cattle counter in the state, unless you get that girl off your mind, you'll not be fit to take charge of the next herd. A trail boss certainly should be able to count his cattle.'

"After that I rushed home, more than a hundred miles by horseback. I arranged a big dance and asked my girl to go along with me. It was customary in those days to take an extra pony along for the girl to ride and her family most always furnished a sidesaddle.

"In my excited state I arrived at her home quite a bit early, saddled my pony for her, and soon we were riding side by side the four miles to the dance. It was a beautiful evening with a full moon which gave me a chance to discuss astronomy instead of matrimony. I talked along until we arrived at the dance when I privately cussed myself out. 'Jack, what makes you such a coward with girls? You are pretty brave in other matters.' I was really disappointed that the first part of the evening was already gone and still I had made no proposal.

"On the way home after the dance, I couldn't rake up courage to propose, even in a roundabout way. When I thought I had put it to her so she could understand, all she would say was, 'This is the finest gaited pony I have ever ridden.' Several times I thought I had brought the subject to a deciding point, but she still praised that pony. I decided to take a desperate measure and play my last card. Of course, I also wanted to play safe. Since I knew the length of the rope on my saddle, I found a tree far enough away from the edge of the bluff we were traveling so I wouldn't take too great a personal risk. I tied one end of the rope to the tree and the other to my neck, crying out in a loud, desperate voice, 'Farewell, cruel world. A good trail boss is making his departure. There seems to be no such word as YES.'

"I played my part in this deception just a little too well, for I was moving pretty rapidly to the end of the rope which by then had nearly jerked my head off. I looked up at Miss Cordie, expecting to see her wringing her hands and in tears, but she was laughing heartily. 'You cowboys are all so funny,' she cried. 'Is that what you call *stretching a rope?*'

"In disgust I pulled myself up, hand over hand, the whole length of the rope, telling myself all the while that since this scheme hadn't worked, I would probably have to wait until fall for her answer. But in the meanwhile, some other cuss might beat me to her, and I sure couldn't stand the thought of that.

"When we arrived at her home, I unsaddled her pony, put the saddle away and said right out loud, 'I'm taking my pony and leaving, or should I have said *our* pony?'

"My girl answered in the softest, sweetest voice, 'Our pony, Jack.'

"I found myself trembling with excitement. I could hardly stammer out my reply. 'Do you mean it?'

"She replied, 'I certainly do, and when shall we set the day?'

"Well, then, I was plumb flustered and instead of kissing my girl, I just kissed the pony who had saved the day for me. I took the rope off his neck, patted him, and said, 'Now, you belong to her, and her home will always be your home.'

"As I rode away and looked back, she still stood there by the pony, waving at me. I laughed to myself when I recalled that my sweet little girl had really never said YES to me."[1]

Jack and his bride, often described as the Belle of Texas, were married on November 11, 1884 in San Antonio. She was delicate and small in stature, hardly reaching to his broad shoulder, her hair still curly and shining as it had been when he first saw her. He often wondered, sometimes out loud, how such a sweet demure little woman could have thrown in her lot with him and put up with the vagaries of a trail driver's life.

Shortly after their marriage Jack moved to the New England Livestock breeding ranch headquarters in Fort Sumner, and later she arrived to set up housekeeping in the old Fort officers' building. Here Jack was made ranch manager, but his career as a trail driver was to continue. They lived in the big adobe house which a number of other families and Mexican servants shared. It had been purchased by the Livestock Company from the Lucien Maxwell estate after his death.

The Potters called this place home until 1893, when the Company sold its holdings and trail driving became a thing of the past. While in residence there, however, Mrs. Potter went back to her girlhood home near Waring, Kendall County, Texas for the birth of their first child, Robert, on November 9, 1885. Gertrude, the first daughter, was also born there, on October 8, 1887, but for the coming of the third child, also a daughter, the mother remained in Fort Sumner. The original fort room where Ethel first opened her eyes on April 6, 1889 was later washed away by the flooding Pecos River.[2]

In 1892 the youngest son, Carl, was born in Kendall County, Texas, but the family home remained in Fort Sumner until 1893. (Since this was written Ethel has died leaving Robert the only surviving child.) Twelve grandchildren enlarged the Potter family, and two of these are now deceased. Jackie—Jack Potter III, son of the eldest child Robert, was named after his grandfather and accompanied him on some of his trips around New Mexico, especially during sessions of the Legislature in Santa Fe.

The geniality and good humor of the father and even temper and kindness of the mother made the Potter family a happy group. All through their long marriage, Jack and Cordie maintained devotion and loyalty to each other. Life was not always easy on the ranch, living conditions were not always convenient, but their situation was typical of the times in which they lived. They were never to be more than modestly well-off, but they were rich in other ways: in friends, respect of the communities where they lived, and a staunch belief and faith that helped them take whatever was their lot.

Jack continued to tell his range stories to whomever would listen, and with the passage of time their true reflection of the era made them a valuable addition to the history of trail-riding days.

Sometime after his courtship and marriage to Miss Cordie, S. Omar Barker of Las Vegas, the noted western author and Potter's friend, wrote a rhymed version of the bashful cowboy's proposal:

JACK POTTER'S COURTIN'[3]

S. Omar Barker

Now young Jack Potter was a man who knowed the way of steers.
From burr-nests in their hairy tails to ticks that chewed their ears;
A Texan and a cow hand, to the saddle bred and born,
He could count a trail herd on the move and never miss a horn.

But one day on a tally, back in eighteen eighty-four,
He got to acting dreamy, and he sure did miss his score.
The Old Man knowed the symptoms. "Jack, you ain't no good like this,
I'll give you just ten days to go and find what is amiss."

A "Miss" was just what ailed him, for he'd fell in love—and stuck—
With sweet Miss Cordy Eddy, fresh from Louisville, Kentuck.
So now Jack rode a hundred miles, a-sweatin' with the thought
Of sweetsome words to ask her with, the way a feller ought:

"I'm just a humble cowhand, Miss Cordie, if you please,
That hereby asks your heart and hand, upon my bended knees."
It sounded mighty simple, thus rehearsed upon the trail,
But when he come to Cordie's house, his words just seemed to fail.

'Twas "Howdy, ma'am" and "How's the crops?" and "How's your Pa?"
But when it came to asking her, he couldn't come to taw.
He took her to a dance one night; the hoss she rode was his.
"He's a dandy little hoss," she says, and "Yep," says Jack, "he is."

They rode home late together and the moon was ridin' high,
And Jack, he got to talkin' about the stars up in the sky,
And how they'd guide a trail herd like they do sea-goin' ships.
But words of love and marriage, they just wouldn't pass his lips.

So he spoke about the pony she was ridin' and he said:
"You'll note he's fancy-gaited, and don't never fight his head."
"He's sure a dandy," she agreed, and heaved a little sigh.
Jack says, "Why you can have him—that is, maybe when I die."

He figured she might savvy what he meant—or maybe guess,
And give him that sweet answer which he hoped for, namely, "Yes."
But when they reached the ranch house he was still a-wonderin' how
He would ever pop the question—and he had to do it now.

Or wait and sweat and suffer 'till the drive was done that fall,
When maybe she'd be married, and he'd lose her after all.
He put away her saddle, led his pony to the gate,
"I reckon I'll be driftin', ma'am, for it is getting late."

Her eyes were bright as star-light and her lips looked sweet as flowers;
Says Jack, "Now, this here pony, is he mine—or is he *ours?*"
"Our pony, Jack," she answered, and her voice was soft as moss.
Then Jack, he claims he kissed her—but she claims he kissed the *hoss!*

23

THE
FORT SUMNER
YEARS

A s trail driving gradually declined, Jack Potter moved into the old Fort Headquarters building on the Pecos River in 1884 to manage the New England Livestock Company. Exactly twenty years previously, in the year of Jack's birth, the fort had been constructed and named for General Edwin Voe Sumner, U.S. Army.

According to the Territorial Records of Incorporation "The New England Livestock Company was a Colorado based corporation chartered by Alfred J. Bacon, Luther C. Coggins, and John Lord of Greeley on November 14, 1881. It was later incorporated in New Mexico on April 9, 1883. W. A. Hinnant and H. E. Hardy of Fort Sumner were appointed as agents 'to represent us and have the management and care of our said business and property in and for the counties of the Territory of New Mexico.' "[1]

In 1883 this corporation, for which young Potter had worked the two previous years as trail boss, had purchased the fort buildings on the Lucien Maxwell estate from representatives of four different cattle companies. Maxwell had purchased these buildings and fort improvements (fences, roads, etc.) from the U.S. Government in 1870, upon the closing of the Navajo encampment there. The property was sold to him for $5,000 at public auction, while the reservation lands were transferred from the War Department to the Secretary of the Interior on April 6, 1871.[2] According to the Territorial Records "there is no evidence that Maxwell owned any of the 38,000 acres which were then apparently public domain, although he probably had a lease on agricultural lands. The later title of the Maxwell family to land appears to be primarily by homestead, also augmented by purchase."[3]

Jack was quite interested in the history of the Maxwell establishment that he was to call home for the next nine years. Many times he expressed his sympathy for the Navajos who were displaced from their lands and relocated amid such unfavorable circumstances. He remarked that the Fort buildings, of which he had personal knowledge, were a failure in every respect as they were made of inferior quality mud adobes. Because they had no foundation, the walls crumbled dangerously and the doors and windows sagged. His description of conditions there, and the succession of ownership of both improvements and surrounding lands, is interesting to the general reader and historians alike.

Years later, in a manuscript titled "Old Fort Sumner," he wrote: "In 1870 the Government sold seven buildings of five rooms each, six of which were capable of housing one hundred men per barracks. In addition to these buildings, there was a hospital, a commissary and Officers' Quarters. There were also fifteen hundred cords of wood, eight hundred bushels of charcoal and numerous other items.

"Lucien B. Maxwell, who had come on a wagon train to Taos and remained to marry Luz Beaubien, daughter of Carlos, and partner in the Beaubien-Miranda Land Grant, was purchaser of the buildings and improvements which he held with a 160 acres squatters' right. The Government reserve of 38,000 acres adjoining the Fort was turned back by the War Department to the Department of the Interior. I have corrected many historians [Potter emphatically states], even the late Ex-Governor Miguel A. Otero in reference to this matter.

"After the Maxwell Estate resold the improvements, livestock, and squatters' rights to four cattlemen in 1883, these individuals began negotiations with the Department of the Interior for the purchase of the 38,000 acres at $1.25 per acre. In a letter to me from Senator Carl Hatch, relying on information given by the Interior Department, it was disclosed that the lands were surveyed, appraised and first offered for public sale on January 15, 1884. The purchasers of the land were Eldridge B. Sopris, Lonny Horn, Sam Doss, Dan L. Taylor and Luther D. Coggins."[4] The same letter also stated that Luz Maxwell had previously sold the improvements to Sam Doss, Lonny Horn, John L. Lord and Dan L. Taylor.

Potter continues, "This group of men, in hack and buckboard with

Charley Wallace as guide, traveled down the Pecos until they reached Fort Sumner. They started at once to negotiate for purchase of the entire spread that was controlled by Dona Luz Maxwell. She put a good price on sheep, cattle, horses, and the ranch. It was claimed that there were two thousand head of cattle, and at that time there were no other cattle on the range at all except the Maxwell herd, branded with a heart on the left ribs or ear-marked with a crop and each ear split. A contract was made and signed with a forfeit put up for security. It was agreed that at a certain date Dona Maxwell and her entire bunch of relatives and helpers on the ranch, of whom there were many, were to give full possession. The new owners then immediately applied for the purchase of the lands to the Department of the Interior through the New Mexico Land Office at Santa Fe.

"It was further agreed among the four purchasers that each was to take a one-fourth interest in the entire ranch and that each would range their cattle separately and under different management. In addition each would have one of the four Officers' Quarters shingle-roof buildings. They would divide the soldiers' barracks, which were constructed with no foundations, for corrals and sheds.

"The new owners procured a surveyor. Water holes were selected and preemption claims filed by the cowboys and Mexicans far out on each side of the ranch to the Tu-les on the Llano Estacado on the east; to the head of the Yeso Creek; and to Mora on the west. They were endeavoring to secure range for fifty thousand head of cattle. Many of the Mexicans who had lived on the Maxwell holdings were retained as helpers and some built claim shacks out on the range. Quite a few were selected to file on 160 acre claims (both homestead and preemption). The managers figured they could well afford to spare Beaver Smith's refreshment parlor where straight whiskey without water was passed over the bar. Old Beaver was given just thirty-six hours to vacate, which he easily managed as all he had to move was a pair of worn poker tables full of bullet holes and a few bottles.

"After the Maxwells gave full possession, Lon Horn was selected from the group to receive and pay for the livestock. The Heart brand (formerly used by Maxwell) was recorded in the name of the New England Livestock Company. It was a holding brand, and the company brand 'F H C' connected **ꟻC** was applied to the increase.

"The only hitch in the entire deal came when Pete Maxwell approached Lonny Horn stating that a horse in the remuda named "Don" was the horse that Billy the Kid rode into Fort Sumner from the Block Ranch in the Capitan Mountains, a full one-hundred-mile stretch, when he escaped after killing his two jailers. He also said that Billy had sent a check for his purchase with the instruction that the horse never be used on the ranch as he was wind-broken from that long hard ride. Pete Maxwell added seriously

Col. Jack Potter's letterhead featured a Harold Bugbee drawing. The steer on the left bears the ⅂C brand of the New England Livestock Company.

that if he sold this particular horse with the other livestock 'Billy, dead these three years, would rise up in his grave and curse me.'

"Horn did not honor Pete's request. Later when I took charge of the New England Livestock Company's ranch, Pete came to me with the same request, adding that he hoped I would use Old Don in my own mount. I did not have the heart to refuse him. I do believe that Don was one of the best horses I ever rode but that was only around camp when I was moving slow. He was so badly wind-broken that he would choke if he traveled any faster than a walk. I kept him for six years until he died at our horse camp on the Mora after drinking too much alkali water.

"Work began in a big way when the new owners took over. Sam Doss drove one herd in from the Driscol ranch in Kansas and another herd was purchased late in the fall in Missouri and shipped as far as Las Vegas, then trailed down to Fort Sumner. In 1884 when I took over, an agent in south Texas bought two large herds of around 3,000 head from Dillard Fant, near San Antonio, and trailed them into our spread. Horn used his Pig Pen ⧺ brand on his cattle, Doss started a new brand with D D Ð one D reversed, burned on the right ribs. Our company received a large mixed herd from south Texas, one from Freer County, now in Oklahoma, and the Tom Yerby herd of the Catholic Cross brand. In 1885 Dan Taylor, one of the new owners, received a herd of 3,000 from Schreiner Brothers near San Antonio, also 3,600 heifer yearlings from Caldwell County, Texas, and the next year, 1886, another herd from the Santa Gertrudes Ranch owned by Captain King. Taylor's new brand was VOX and VO. This completed the stocking of the New England ranch at Fort Sumner.

"In 1885, I believe, Fort Sumner was the most important inland town in eastern New Mexico. Some of the herds that trailed through there came from the lower Pecos and Big Bend country of Texas, and were driven to western New Mexico and Arizona, crossing the old Goodnight-Loving Trail at Fort Sumner. The trail that continued into Arizona was the Jim Stinson Trail that began in about 1882. It branched off from the Western Trail at Albany, followed up to Matador, then crossed the Texas Panhandle to Portales Spring in New Mexico, on to Fort Sumner on the Pecos. From the river, a trail led to the Estancia valley. Another branch dipped down to Socorro and took a southwesterly direction into Arizona. The cattle trailed over this route were mostly those that belonged to the New Mexico Land and Cattle Company which branded two circles (O O). It was headed by Joel P. Whitney of San Francisco. Stinson and Metcalf managed the Estancia ranch held by this company and trailed their cattle west. The Stinson cowboys were a bunch of fast riding cutups, involved in gun fights and at least one murder. Metcalf had to discharge them all after the roundup of 1887.

"We did not always use the Goodnight–Loving trail from Fort Sumner, especially during drought times, when parched grass and dry water holes took a murderous toll. The constant lowing of thirst-maddened cattle brought nightmares to cowboys already hollow-eyed from lack of sleep. I helped blaze a new trail off the beaten path that started from the Brazil and Maxwell ranches on the Taiban on that long, dry stretch of eighty miles to the "Blue Holes" on the Pajarita, up to the plains at Peet Canyon via Aqua Caballo and off the plains several miles east to the Cuneva ranch."[5]

Jack Potter was too busy with the problems of the New England Livestock Company to be much concerned with the circumstances that beset herds going up the Western Trail into Kansas to Dodge in 1884 and 1885. Because of the growing menace to northern cattle from Texas tick fever, Kansas prohibited the herds from entering the state. A National Trail, established through the auspices of the U.S. Government, branched off at Woodward, Oklahoma, passed through the upper Texas Panhandle, crossed No Man's Land, and followed up the Kansas boundary just inside eastern Colorado. The entire state of Kansas was thus bypassed; the trail entered Nebraska to meet various shipping points along the Union Pacific Railroad.

Frank King wrote concerning this emergency in trail driving: "Them ticks sure did make the Kansas cattle sick, but it wasn't as bad as represented on account of a heap of the country was wide open with no cattle grazing. The driveway as designated included three miles of government land, adjoining the state line and three miles just inside the Colorado state line."[6]

In June 1885, however, Jack did drive a herd for his company with Ogalalla, Nebraska as the destination. On the way up he was met by a messenger sent by the town of Dodge City to tell all drovers that the quarantine recently enacted, resulting in the formation of the National Trail, had been investigated by attorney Mike Sutton and was based on an old law that had never been enforced.[7]

Potter told his messenger, "Well, it seems as if every old waddy in Texas that could borrow a dollar has invested in cattle this year to speculate on the Kansas market. To my knowledge there are 400,000 head on the trail now. There'll be hell to pay."

During the next two weeks as many as ten herds traveled a little north of west. After Potter arrived at Miles Camp, just above Point of Rocks on the Kansas line, they lay over for a few days to let some of the crush pass on. Jack knew that where there were too many herds pressed together there was danger of mixing, especially in stormy weather. If such happened, it was tedious to separate them again and brought much cussing and hard riding to the point and swing men.

Just as Dodge City had superseded Abilene as the cowboy capital and shipping center for trail herds, so did Trail City on the state line between Kansas and Colorado become the mecca for the cow trade. This was the direct result of the Kansas quarantine and the blazing of the National Trail. No other such town sprang up farther west, because after two years most of the cattlemen shipped herds by railroad instead of driving. A new era had begun.

The New England Company owned three other ranches besides the spread at Fort Sumner. They maintained a maturing ranch at Cheyenne, Wyoming, and another on the Tongue River in Montana, where the company trailed its herds to be shipped after the Burlington Railroad had extended west. Their south Texas ranch was still the source of much of the cattle that came through to Fort Sumner and on north. In 1886 they were trailing a short distance to Las Vegas to the railhead which had been established by the Santa Fe, and in 1887 they also trailed up the eastern grasslands of New Mexico to Springer to load cattle there.

By 1878 Texas had two rail connections through branch lines to the Chicago beef market, and after 1880, other lines extended West as well. In New Mexico between 1877 and 1881, the Santa Fe Railroad ran from Raton to El Paso. The New England Company, like other Texas cattle producers, was slow to adapt to rail shipping.[8] Costs of transportation, plus feed during the journey, were unattractive to these hardy drovers who had learned how to profit by crossing the grassy plains of west Texas and eastern New Mexico. Some maintained their records showed that 1,500 to 3,000 head, an average herd, could be trailed more cheaply than shipped. Time was not too pressing a factor to the cowboy of this area. Life was exciting and had its rewards in monthly celebrations in little cow towns scattered around the ranges. Cattlemen also maintained that losses were greater through faulty handling by the railway hands than by trailing although nature, in the form of storms, stampedes, and normal trail losses, took its toll.[9]

In addition cattle owners objected to paying the railroads in advance, as they were accustomed to settling with their drovers and cowboys after the herd was finally sold. Stockmen had to maintain permanent crews, regardless of the way cattle were marketed, and they continued to trail herds as long as they could. When barbed wire, settlers, and additional rail lines made droving finally impractical, the owners used a combination of trailing and shipping, as Potter himself employed on the New England spread.

Owners and drovers alike were sorry to see the old ways end. George Burrows of Del Rio, Texas once sadly remarked, "I put in 18–20 years on the trail and all I had in final outcome was a pair of high heeled boots, striped pants, and $4.80 worth of assorted clothing—so there you are." But he also said that he'd do it all over if the chance came.[10]

Joseph McCoy, the ingenious businessman and cattle trader who had first promoted a shipping dock in Abilene, Kansas as early as 1867, stated that refrigerated cars, originated at this time, could accommodate a daily slaughter of 500 head of cattle. This easy way of preserving the meat also contributed to the collapse of the cattle driving industry. In addition, the rush for quick profits resulted in overstocking and overgrazing of the western ranges; homesteaders criticized the illegal use of public lands and the extra-legal leasing of Indian lands. State quarantine laws became more rigid. The winter of 1885–86, followed by drought, exacted an enormous toll, which was even greater in the following years when increased losses led to the final collapse of open range ranching.[11]

Potter realized how changes in the cattle industry were making themselves felt on the New England spread. The heavy calf increase, droughts, blizzards, short grass, and low prices were all factors in the company's decision to gradually liquidate. Three of the owners closed out their stock interest and the ranch land itself was put up for sale. After the property was disposed of to various buyers, the famous old Fort, now unoccupied except for the ghosts of history, began to crumble. The largest building of fifteen rooms where the Maxwells had lived, including the room in which Billy the Kid was shot, was salvaged by Lon Horn, who took the lumber to build a new ranch house at the Tu-les, thirty miles up the way on the old Portales Road.

Later a flood cut into the east bank of the Pecos, taking away all the old landmarks as the thick red current rushed southward to Horsehead Crossing in Texas, which was marked by bleached skulls stuck on posts. As there was no foundation to many of the adobe buildings, not much was left that could be identified as a marker. The last time Jack Potter visited the place he found nothing to indicate where so much history had taken place and where he had spent those happy and profitable years from 1884 to 1894 with the New England Livestock Company.

FROM THE PECOS TO THE DRY CIMARRON

By the time Jack Potter had spent ten years as manager of the New England Livestock Company's maturing ranch at Fort Sumner, that area of bad water, windstorms, and sand dunes had lost some of its fascination for him. Billy the Kid and two of his gunmen were filling six-foot spaces in the old Boothill Cemetery near the river. Beaver Smith, the saloon keeper, and his shoot'em-up friends had left to seek their fortunes elsewhere. The Lincoln County War had ended, and the vast empire of cattleman John Chisum had broken up under mismanagement after his death. In fact, the rough cattle country had settled down so much that cowmen began to associate with their formerly scorned contemporaries—the sheep herders. Sometimes, if financially pinched, cowmen even borrowed cash from their avowed rivals of the range.

After a three years' drought, Potter's company liquidated its herd and put the majority of its cattle on the trail to northern markets. When some of the small operators around the Fort Sumner area decided to pool their herds and migrate to the Cimarron Valley near the New Mexico–Oklahoma boundary, he made the decision to go with them. During the earlier trailing days, Jack had become familiar with this fine grass country and knew it to be a favorable location. In 1894 a group consisting of four Potter brothers

and their families, Jack's, Bill's, John's, and Temple's, made the move.
Two other men, James and Charles Wiggins, and their families also came
along. They settled in the neutral two-mile strip of "No Man's Land," a
haven for cowmen because of fresh spring water and tall grass in a free
range with no taxes to pay.

This area was also a refuge for outlaws since there was no legal juris-
diction over the strip, which had first been set aside by the U.S. Government as an outlet for the Indian tribes to cross to New Mexico hunting
grounds from their reservation. The true western boundary of the strip
was the 103rd meridian, which divided Oklahoma from New Mexico. The
approximate two-mile difference between the 103rd meridian boundary
and the boundary claimed by Texas as legal was caused by an error in the
original survey. Ordered by the government in 1859, the surveyor, John
Clark, ran a line at the southwest corner of Texas northward to establish
the New Mexico border at the northwest corner of Texas. He completed
only the southern part of the line, however; then, after an interruption of
activities due to extremely hot, dry weather, he began his survey from
the northern end. The lines failed to coincide by nearly two miles, thus
creating a "jog" in the New Mexico–Oklahoma and New Mexico–Texas
north–south boundary.[1] Neither New Mexico nor Oklahoma claimed this
strip. Before the error was discovered, the results of the survey were
accepted as correct by the Department of the Interior. Later, even though
the mistake was revealed, the Capital Syndicate (XIT) Company, which
built the Texas state capitol, was able to have the survey declared correct
on March 4, 1891.[2]

Since New Mexico was not yet admitted into the Union, the question
of the boundary was not resolved until February 16, 1911 by a Joint Resolution of Congress.[3] Small wonder that this neutral area filled up with
squatters, outlaws, saloon keepers, and cattle rustlers, as there were no
taxes and no laws.

Since a homestead could be claimed by squatter's rights, a large group,
the Potter family and their acquaintances, held land as squatters until
1900. It was very difficult to get action from Washington, even though
petitions asking for information and a correct survey had been sent many
times. It took a killing or two to get results.

The Potter families lived under the ruling and laws of No Man's Land
that had been formulated by the first group that invaded the territory in
1886, establishing Beaver City, Oklahoma as the capital, with a Dr. Lindly
as spokesman. He appointed an advisory board of six men to rule the area.[4]
One of the chief concerns was protection for the individual squatter and his
land. Since there was no demand for labor, many men had to seek work
elsewhere, but they never left their claims without first marking them well

with a plowed furrow around the 160 acres. Some even made sod and grass monuments at each corner to show their boundaries. The penalty for jumping a squatter's claim was certain death if the violator was caught. A bunch of armed "regulators" handled such cases in their own areas.[5]

Lindly appointed a justice of the peace for each community to hear minor offenses, issue marriage certificates, and perform ceremonies. The colony's success encouraged others to come to No Man's Land, but most of them stopped at the eastern border, where the terrain was more adapted to farming.

Another civilizing influence occurred with the arrival in 1888 of the Fort Worth and Denver Railroad at Clayton, New Mexico, just fifteen miles over the line from the "Strip." A mercantile store was established by a Mr. Hubbard, who ordered weekly supplies along with the mail which was delivered from Trinidad, Colorado. Not long after the arrival of the Potters and a number of other families, the need for a post office nearer home was discussed at a meeting of settlers and cowboys. Mr. Hubbard was chosen to be the designated postmaster, and the name of his daughter Florence suggested as the name of the new postal station. The petition was granted by the Post Office Department. Later the name was changed from Florence to Kenton.[6]

One of the saloons that served the new community was also near Mr. Hubbard's store. Only a mile farther down the road another bartender set up as a competitor, and neither of them suffered from lack of trade. The situation grew pretty rough, with fist fights, knifings, and shoot'em ups on a regular basis, until the women organized their own vigilante committee and set fire to the saloon near Hubbard's, giving orders to the other to move on or suffer the consequences of feminine ire.

Kenton grew with the establishment of another store by merchant F. B. Drew. In a short while the little town boasted two churches, a bank, and a hotel which Jack Potter ran for a while. Mr. Drew knew how to appeal to his customers, and in order to attract new trade, he built a large dance hall onto his store that was used for community meetings and dances. In a column later written for the *Union County Leader*, Jack Potter humorously related some of the happenings at a dance at Drew's store.

"One night, Lin Masker, a mischief-making cowboy caused a near riot among the women folk attending the dance. Because many of them had brought their young children, even small babies, with them, it was necessary to use a storage space under the sale counter to put the children to sleep during the dance. Well, Lin thought as how it wouldn't hurt none to just mix up these children a bit and silently moved them around from the places where the mothers had laid them down to sleep. When folks were ready to go home, the women began to pick up the wrong babies, scrambling for them under the tumbled blankets and quilts. There was a heap of screaming and scratching with some women grabbing babies out of each other's arms with cries of "kidnap, kidnap" before the confusion was straightened out and each woman claimed her rightful child. Lin had to hide out for a few days after that fiasco."[7]

The Potter family was happily established on a place which Jack named Rancho Escondido or Hidden Ranch. It was located on a dry arroyo of the Cimarron River in New Mexico just across the state line from the town of Kenton, Oklahoma. According to Ethel, the youngest daughter, they usually walked the mile and a half to school and attended church services there also. Each weeknight the devout mother conducted prayer and Bible reading for the children, and their father approved of the family worship, participating when he was at home. This delicate little mother also attended to all the discipline for the children, not hesitating to turn them "over her lap" if need be. Their father, Ethel said, seemed just too good-natured and softhearted to assume this part of the childrens' upbringing.[8]

Besides rearing her own brood, Mrs. Potter also was foster mother to a number of runaway boys who drifted by their place. Many of the boys were orphans, some came from broken homes, while others had simply run away to seek their fortunes in the West. According to Ethel her mother cared for at least seven or eight boys from eight to sixteen years of age that she could remember, besides countless others who just stopped by for food and overnight shelter. A religious woman herself, Mrs. Potter exacted discipline and church attendance from these temporary sons of the household. The father was generous in outfitting them with warm clothing from a store in Kenton in which he had an interest. If he could, he supplied them with enough cash to get them on their way to the next layover on their wanderings. Some stayed to help the Potters with the chores around the ranch for several months. One boy in particular remained with them so long that he seemed part of the family.[9]

This boy, Alfred H. Phillips, nicknamed "Smokey," later wrote an account detailing the events leading up to his arrival in Kenton. He was staying with a family named Tooker who had three adopted children, including himself, while they lived in Marion, Kansas. When the Tookers moved to New Mexico north of Clayton, Alfred, then about fifteen, felt that he was ready to be "on his own." He confided his plans to leave his adoptive parents to a friend called Ed, and this boy agreed to go along with him.

"Smokey" Phillips later wrote: "I saw Ed one day and told him that I was leaving right away, the following Sunday, and that I would be near Currumpa Creek about the middle of the afternoon. At the appointed time when I saw Ed coming, I got off Tooker's pony, took his bridle and hung it on the saddle horn, tying it securely, and gave him a slap on the rump to start him back home.

"My friend was pretty well outfitted with clothes as he had on a good suit, shoes, socks, and underwear. All my worldly goods consisted of the clothes on my back, a ragged pair of knee pants, blue workshirt, and torn straw hat, no shoes, socks, or underwear. I was fifteen and had never worn shoes in the summertime or had a pair of long breeches.

"We started out walking, and by a light in the darkness made our way to a Mexican sheep camp where we were fed frijoles and tortillas that filled us up pretty good. Since the moon was up, we walked a while longer, resting in between stretches. We kept this up all night, until about dawn we stopped by a dugout where a man living alone gave us breakfast. We did not tell him who we were or where we were going. We were relieved that he did not ask. Pretty soon we struck the trail again.

"Late in the afternoon of the next day, we saw the roof of a house just over a low hill, so we headed toward it. Two women homesteaders with a bunch of children were sharing a house together while their husbands were away at work. They were nice to us, gave us food, and allowed us to spend the night.

"About midmorning of our third day on the road, we saw a wagon driven by a man I later knew as Eb Cochran. He was on the way to Clayton to see a dentist, but he advised us to stay on the road until we reached Kenton. 'Then,' he said, 'when you arrive, ask for Jack Potter. You'll know him, for he's the biggest man in town, tall, heavyset, and wears a white, wide-brimmed Stetson.'

"As we came into Kenton, we saw a boy about my age standing downtown. When we asked him about Potter, he told us that he would help us find him, but first he asked us to come home with him, spend the night, and have breakfast the next morning. We were sure glad. His father, Charles Wiggins, owned the Kenton Hotel then. About midmorning Charlie pointed out a man standing in front of a small store building. 'That's him, that's Jack Potter.'

"We walked over to him and I asked, looking way up because he was so tall, 'Are you Mr. Potter?' He smiled, looked down at me, and answered that he was the man and what did we want of him. I came right out and asked for a job, but I didn't tell him I had run away. I told him that Ed and I were both farm boys used to hard work and that we would do anything he could find for us. We were sure relieved when he answered, 'I think I can use you two. Come in the store with me.'

"Ed and I followed him out of the bright summer light into the dim coolness of the store. I thought it had more goods in it than I had ever seen before, even though it was a small building. Mr. Potter stopped by a rack of work pants and shirts. He looked at us and smiled. 'One of you fellers seems like he's in pretty bad shape. We'll start with him first.' Then he turned to me to ask, 'Where's the rest of your belongings?'

"I was ashamed to admit that I had nothing else to my name. I hung my head and scraped my bare feet across the smooth plank floor. But he sure made me smile when he outfitted me with work pants, shoes, a change of underwear, and socks, and a Stetson that bore a $3.00 price tag on it. Then he sent me back into the warehouse to change into my new clothes. I was sure puffed up and pleased. We stood around a few more minutes and I guess he saw me eyeing some leather hatbands hanging from a rack. Without a word, he reached over, took the band down, handed it to me, and said, 'Here, if you want to be a cowboy, you'll need this.' I'll never forget how proud I was at that moment. Nothing I have ever had since that time has given the pleasure that that leather hatband gave to me, just a runaway orphan boy.

"Mr. Potter fixed up Ed with some things too, but he didn't need as much as I. When we went outside the store, he pointed down the road towards his ranch house, saying, 'Go on down this road about two miles until you reach my house. Go inside and tell Mrs. Potter that I sent you. Tell her to give you a good feed and put you both to work. And that is how I came to the Dry Cimarron ranch of Jack Potter in August, 1911.'"[10]

The other boy, Ed, nicknamed "Sandy," stayed a while then moved on, but Smokey remained much longer, working around the ranch at odd jobs, tending the cattle, and mending fences. When the house became more crowded, Smokey was told that he would have to go to a ranch home that Mrs. Potter had located for him. At the appointed time he was to leave, Smokey was nowhere to be found until someone discovered him, crying his heart out behind the door of a bedroom.

No wonder Smokey wanted to stay. The Potters had good times together. Most of the family were musically inclined and enjoyed singing in the living room around the old pump organ that Mrs. Potter played on occasion. Ethel later recalled that her mother and her Uncle John Potter especially enjoyed singing together, and that they had "real good voices."[11]

As in all rural communities, the school was the source of entertainment as well as education. There were "literary" programs given at intervals in which the pupils took part by saying speeches and acting in plays. "My dad usually wound up the program by telling some of his tall tales," commented Ethel, smiling at the memory. "People never seemed to tire of listening to his stories of old trail days. Sometimes he'd 'stretch the blanket' a little by exaggerating, but everyone knew that most of what he said was true."[12]

In the winter of 1911 Jack Potter lost all of his cattle in a blizzard, as did other ranchers in the Cimarron Valley. After this the family saw hard times for awhile, but their chief needs of food and shelter were met and they managed as well as they could. Mrs. Eddy, Cordie Potter's mother, lived with them a number of years, helping with the cooking and sewing for the growing children. In this way the mother was free to help her neighbors in times of emergency and illness, as every ranch wife was accustomed to do. People survived by sharing and helping others in case of need. When the call came, Mrs. Potter was always ready, even though she herself did not enjoy robust health.

Everyone in the Valley knew the Potters, and the children of neighbors and friends were especially fond of the kindhearted father who told stories and shared treats from his store. Ethel later recalled that once he passed the Kenton school ground with a barrel of apples in his wagon on the way to his store. "We kids ran out and begged until he gave everyone in school an apple, leaving very few to take back to his store. But he was always like that, generous with whatever he had."[13]

Holidays were long anticipated and preparations were the source of much activity around the Rancho Escondido. In a column for the *Union County Leader* many years later, Potter described one of the celebrations: "I remember one Christmas when we commenced two weeks ahead of time to haul in the holiday wood, corral the turkey so it would grow fine and fat, hung up a beef in the smokehouse, and salted down a large hog, including mixing up a batch of spicy ground sausage. Besides all this fine food, one day the mail carrier brought in a whiskey jug from Charles Meredith of Clayton which was labeled 'Escondido Cowboys with my compliments and Holiday Greetings.'

"With all this food on hand, my wife and I each decided to invite our own friends to share Christmas dinner with us. She invited A. C. Thompson, known as Pa Thompson, and his family. He was a religious feller who was given to long prayers and blessings at the table. My guests were a bunch of middle-aged, old-time cowboys whom I had known on the range. They would not come up to the house until dinner was announced as they preferred to stay at the barn telling stories and getting full of Christmas cheer from Charley's jug. When we sat down to eat, Pa Thompson began to discourse and argue his religion and humiliate the old boys who just sat there stuffing food and being quiet in an effort to keep him from smelling their breaths.

"The next day my wife commented that my guests didn't behave very well, and she thought that there must have been 'some liquor on the premises which they had gotten into before dinner was served.'

" 'Well,' I answered, 'I just can't help that. It's entirely possible that there *was* some liquor down at the barn.'

"Later I spoke to one of the cowboys about my wife noticing and being embarrassed before Pa Thompson and his family. He answered me by saying, 'That's just too bad. Look at this label written on the jug that came from Charley Meredith. It's written in pencil. Why not rub out Escondido cowboys and write A. C. Thompson in its place?' So that's what he did and then laid the jug in a hen's nest where one of the children would be sure to find it.

"In a little while I noticed my two boys carrying the jug back to the house, trying not to let any one see it as they hid it between them. I was sure that they would show it to their mother and that someone was bound to have trouble. But I didn't say anything to her about it. Later, when the children were out of the house, she remarked, 'Did you know that Brother Thompson DRANK?'

"I answered, 'Not to my knowledge, I can't believe that he does. You'll have to prove it to me.'

" 'Well, I have the evidence,' she said. 'The boys found an empty jug with his name on it in the hen's nest.'

" 'Perhaps it was just a water jug,' I countered.

"She produced the jug, pulled the cork and made me smell it. 'Does that smell like water to you?' she asked impatiently.

"All I can say is that eventually my wife found out that we had played a joke on her and Brother Thompson, and it cost me a new piano and a summer vacation to her folks in Texas to get back in good graces."[14]

Ranchers in the early days of the Strip or No Man's Land had their own ways of solving problems, usually with ingenuity and humor. Because of the 160-mile distance from the state line across Beaver County, Oklahoma to the county seat where court was held, ranchers did not like to take the necessary time off to travel there to answer jury summons. In New Mexico the nearest court was at Springer, which was also too far away for easy transportation. After a particularly trying experience in snowdrifts and cold wind, the ranchers devised a scheme to avoid court duty if at all possible.

County officers knew of this objection on the part of the ranchers and would try to slip up to a headquarters or roundup and catch the cowboys on the spot with a summons. A signal was therefore arranged between them to alert passersby that a sheriff was in the vicinity and to lay low until he passed on. A bleached cow head was simply hung on a fence as a notice to all who wanted to avoid jury duty that they should stay out of sight. This was then taken down on a later day. It worked a special hardship on the Kenton Hotel where all the ranchers stayed and put up their teams, for trade was mighty slim until that old beef skull was removed and the coast was clear again.[15]

There was not much social life for the women except that associated with either church or school or occasional dances. They all had large families that required most of their attention, and they accepted their lot as the hub of family life which allowed little time for recreation. Men in Kenton

"A bleached cow head was simply hung on a fence as a notice to all."

not only hung around the stores and saloons; they organized a lodge called the MWA, which caused quite a stir with its initiations. The same Drew warehouse that served as a dance hall was rented as a temporary lodge room. The officers were swamped with applications for membership from ranchers and merchants alike. It seemed that the initiation ceremony had aroused community curiosity, as did the pass word and the general secrecy surrounding the organization.

There was a wooden goat on wheels with a handle fastened behind, which could move the goat and its hapless rider in any direction and at any speed the initiators chose to employ. Since the men were all ranchers, their plans for initiation were related to the cattle industry, something that everyone understood and would not object to. Examining ears for ticks, rough handling of lips and gums to determine age by teeth, a simulated branding by application of heated iron to a piece of bacon slab held to the candidate's hindquarters, caused much apprehension to those who could smell the smoke or who peeped through the bullet holes in the door to watch the goings on.

One fellow who was especially nervous threatened the initiators by saying, "If you men apply that branding iron, I'll meet you sometime when you are not expecting it, and you will smell plenty of powder smoke about your head."

Another one argued, "Why don't you use a smaller iron? You know that I make my living by riding in the saddle all day, and I'm not able to take the time out lying around the ranch waiting for that there brand to heal."

Even the wives put up objections to the initiation ceremonies, because they couldn't get their husbands to divulge the secrets or tell them the password. Some resorted to locking their men out of the house on lodge nights and opening up only when the password was revealed.[16]

Life was rough, humor was horseplay, and the squeamish had to take what was handed out to them. Jack Potter was always in the thick of things and commented later that to see middle-aged men cavorting around in such ridiculous postures and activities was one of the "greatest pleasures" of his life.

The Potter family continued to live at the Escondido Ranch for a number of years. The children were now married and Jack and his devoted wife were ready for an easier life. The years on the ranch had been profitable. Jack had made a comeback after the blizzard of 1911, and though never a big operator he had made a comfortable living for his family, as there had been a steady demand for beef at good prices.

The situation began to gradually change, however, in the middle 1920s. At that time Jack was about sixty years of age and beginning to think of a less strenuous occupation. Just before the crash of 1929 he concluded the sale transactions on the ranch property and moved into Clayton.

This was fortunate timing for Jack Potter, for due to depression and financial stress, both nationwide and in northeastern New Mexico, the ranch changed owners several times in the next few years. Mrs. D. H. Haley, formerly of Clayton but now of Portales, recalls that her father, Roy Wright, owned the Potter ranch after the crash of 1929. The property was later bought by Raymond Huff.

CLAYTON'S
COLORFUL CITIZEN

In Clayton Jack and Cordie Potter lived in a two-story stucco and frame house that was later remodeled into apartments. There were now grandchildren to brighten their lives and to listen to Jack's stories of trailing days. Ethel and her husband, George Wade, lived at the end of the same block. Well thought of and respected, the Potters fitted well into small town life, becoming "pillars" in the Methodist church with consistent Sunday attendance and participation in all church affairs. Jack was a loyal supporter of his lodge as well.

About the time of their move to Clayton, Jack entered a contest sponsored by the *Pioneer State Tribune* on early-day events in which he wrote from actual experience. He placed second, and surprisingly this was the beginning of a new part-time career for him. Although he had always been loquacious and a humorous storyteller, he had not had sufficient formal education to enable him to embark on a writing career without extensive editorial assistance. At the editor's request, however, he did jot down his recollections, which were edited and published in the *Union County Leader*. His column added to his already wide town and county recognition and attracted readers of a younger generation. It added to his reputation and might have won a few votes in his first election to the

House of Representatives of the New Mexico Legislature in the fall of 1932.

The per diem pay of legislators was only five dollars. Sometimes it was hard in a small ranching community to find capable men who were willing and financially able to take the necessary time to campaign for office and attend sessions. Because Jack Potter was personable, had a host of friends, and at age sixty-eight had the health and time to devote to it, he was approached to run on the Democratic ticket. His biggest asset politically, however, was his friendship among the Spanish-speaking citizenry of Union County. He had spoken their language since his trail-riding days in south Texas. He knew their habits and preferences in voting, and his supporters felt he could count on their siding with him on a close vote. Since politics is often the "power of persuasion," Jack Potter's genial manner and impressive appearance, with well-trimmed moustache and great bulk, made him an attractive candidate. His honesty and reputation for fair dealing also aided the victory he won at the polls in the primary and general elections of 1932.

When he arrived in the capital for the Legislative session, he threatened to pitch his "Camp Coyote" on the Santa Fe River rather than pay the seven dollars daily charge at the La Fonda Hotel. He stayed with his Spanish friends, however, and in this way he became more closely aligned with an impressive block of votes. This helped win a very significant roll call affecting the financial status of state schools.

The ad valorem tax generously supported the schools prior to 1934, but because of the nationwide depression, school operations were restricted as tax payments declined. A group of educators led by Raymond Huff of Clayton, Chairman of the State Board of Education; Richard Grissom, State Budget Auditor; and John Milne, Superintendent of Albuquerque Schools, supported an emergency two-percent sales tax for school operation.

Having only limited education himself, Potter was convinced by Huff of the great need for this tax measure. The citizens of Union and Harding Counties aligned with Superintendent Huff and Potter to a large extent in spite of hard times. Elsewhere over the state, there was much less support.

The Eleventh Session of the New Mexico Legislature saw many a stormy debate. The committee advocating passage strove to obtain every favorable vote. Huff knew his fellow townsman Potter could be counted on to bring in a number of votes from the Spanish community. The situation in hotels and bars of Santa Fe was tense that weekend; Potter spent his time persuading his Spanish amigos. When the final vote was taken, the measure was approved. This "earmarked" school tax, as it was called in true cattleman terminology, succeeded in putting the schools on a sound basis as long as it remained in effect.[1]

Potter was returned to the Legislature for two more sessions. In one of these, 1936, a special appointment by Governor Clyde Tingley gave him

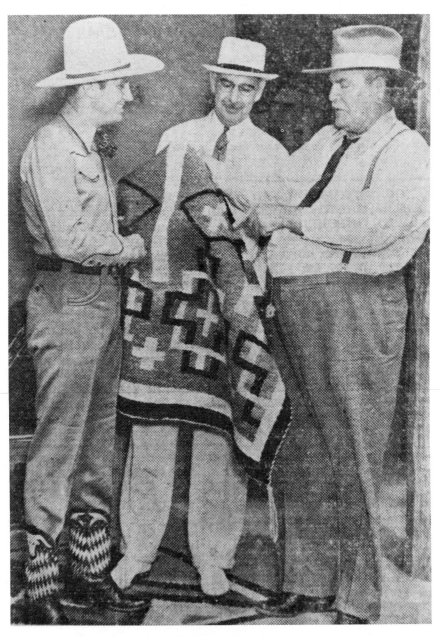

Lead Steer Potter (right) presents Navajo blanket to Gene Autry (left) while Maury Maverick looks on. Photographed at the Texas Centennial by the Dallas Morning News, *1936.*

the honorary title of Colonel, Aide de Camp. Jack was immensely proud of this title and used it on his letterhead and to sign his stories as well. Townspeople and friends over the state subsequently referred to him as Colonel. Generally he signed his name with the title abbreviated, Col. Jack Potter, but others used the formal full spelling—Colonel. He was also appointed official state representative to the Texas Centennial in Dallas, 1936, the first person to receive such an appointment.

While he was at the Centennial Potter had the opportunity to present Gene Autry, the "Singing Cowboy," a handsome Navajo rug from the state of New Mexico. They posed together on the porch of the reproduction of the Governor's Palace of Santa Fe which housed the New Mexico exhibits. Autry, it turned out, was a genuine cowboy who had become a popular singer. He told Potter of his youthful experiences when he worked on a farm and ranch near Clovis. He had learned to sing while working around the cattle and gained Jack's admiration with his genuine "real cowboy" background and manners. Perhaps Jack was also pleased because Gene Autry seemed a willing listener to some of his yarns of the trail. After hearing a few "big windies," Autry remarked that Potter "sure knew his longhorns and lead steers."

When Autry asked Potter if cattle knew the difference between good singing and bad, Jack related a story of how he was almost fired because the cattle didn't like the noise he made, which, according to the boss, almost "threw them into a mill." The next morning he was relieved of the night watch and put in charge of the remuda, with the wrangler watching and singing to the herd. "At least I didn't lose my job, but I never had no use for that herd after that," he remarked. In their last conversation at the exhibit, Gene Autry told Potter, "I envy you having all those experiences on the trail. I believe that I too would have fitted in on long cattle drives."[2]

Potter served three terms in the New Mexico Legislature, and was chairman of the Penitentiary Committee and a member of the Banking, Educational, Livestock, Labor, and Public Land Committees. His experiences with cattle and ranching problems stood him in good stead on his legislative work, which he enjoyed in spite of occasional complaints.

In a newspaper column he later expressed the frustrations that lawmakers have suffered from time immemorial. He complained that he was "a target for newspapers," accused of selling out his constituents, and that he was particularly attacked by the old Townsendites (followers of Dr. Townsend who advocated government pay of $200 per month for every old person). He declared that only young men who might use their experience in the Legislature as a stepping-stone to higher office received any benefit from serving as a county representative or senator.

Potter also described the general improvement of the tone of the legislative proceedings when the time-consuming rereading of a bill in Spanish was discontinued. He accused some of the proponents of this practice of using the time for sleeping and catching up from too much partying the night before.[3]

With characteristic humor, Potter wrote his impressions of the social life of Santa Fe:

> I will always remember the time I attended a reception at the Governor's Mansion during Arthur Seligman's term. Some of the legislators had ordered dress suits, possibly to impress the four women members of that session. Representative Nancy Lane of Santa Fe had been reared and highly educated in the East. In marked contrast another Representative was a plump, young countrywoman who was fully prepared to create as much attention as Nancy. The night of the reception she came up to me, with a ten-foot train of satin draped over her arm, and said in a coquettish way, "Col. Jack, you're always talking in cow language. Would you say that I look like a prize Hereford yearling tonight?" I was plumb taken by surprise, but I told her that she looked more like a mature Jersey, the five-gallon a day type, than any yearling I had ever seen.[4]

Jack also attended the traditional Governor's reception during John Miles' first term. In the splendor of the formal halls, he saw "two old cow waddies, Burton Roach and George Armijo, dressed up in black evening suits. I told them they sure looked out of place in those outfits." I think that the poorest dressed man in all of Santa Fe was James Hinkle when he was Governor. He looked like he had just come in off the range most of the time, but hard riding when he was young had given him a nice spread between the knees."[5]

Such descriptive phrases as Jack employed in his conversation also sprinkled his writings, which began to appear more regularly in his hometown paper. He turned in a weekly column, the subjects evidently of his own choosing. His stories were carefully edited, but not condensed, by the several editors who dealt with his work. From about 1935 to 1945 he authored dozens of articles describing his trail experiences and many historical events. His memory was better than his grammar and spelling; there were very few, if any, times that he was not correct in what he recalled. His columns served to bring to a younger reading public the colorful career he had followed and the way the building of communities at a shipping point or trade center was begun.

In an undated clipping from one of his scrapbooks he tells of the development of Clayton, beginning in 1888:

> . . . two railway construction companies from both north and south directions met at the lake side camp which became Clayton. This was

the last link to be finished in the Colorado and Southern Railway Company. The end of construction put many men and teams out of work and a committee was appointed to confer with the rail people to establish a town at this same site. Senator S. W. Dorsey, who controlled extensive grazing areas and was known to be a real promoter, was called upon to help. Acting upon his advice, a representative was sent to Santa Fe to procure a "forty acre scrip" and to organize an independent town site company. Tom Holland surveyed the proposed site. Mr. Shaddox and Perrin began to sell town lots and were encouraged when Dorsey moved in a ranch house and a barn from his property to the proposed town to be used as a hotel. He donated this property and let it be known that he would be amply rewarded if the new town was named CLAYTON after his son.

Soon the doors of the hotel were swinging wide for trade. Dorsey also arranged for a twenty thousand dollar stock of merchandize to be shipped in to open a general mercantile store. This was the beginning of the Fox Bros. and Bushnell Mercantile Co. John Hill was appointed to ride out to the ranges and seek committments for cattle shipment from the newly established Clayton. The local saloons even furnished him with a five gallon jug of whiskey to use as a persuader.

This sort of promotion began to put Clayton on the map. Cattle, sheep and sheared wool were shipped in large quantities to be stored at first in a long room at the north end of the depot. As soon as possible other private storage houses were erected along the right of way. As a result of the rapid expansion in the new town, Folsom and Texline began to decline."[6]

Jack Potter recorded many of the events and the men who had left a special mark on the community of Clayton. One man in particular, his black friend Spencer Graves, is worthy of mention. "Negro Spence," as Potter referred to him, came in 1900 to file and prove up on a homestead adjoining the Clayton townsite just north of town. "In those days," Potter wrote,

Negroes were barred from living in Clayton unless they were servants for prominent townspeople. Chris Otto had old Frank as his handy man, the Eklunds had old Gene, Doc Slack was raising a Negro boy named Buddy, and the Lackeys had a fellow named King. Negro Spence and his wife Etta lived in town also because Etta was a good cook. Spence eked out a living blacking shoes on a downtown street.

Spence had many friends among the men who came to his shoe-shine stand. He liked to talk religion and politics to anyone who would listen. He became determined to build a Negro Baptist Church and spent several years soliciting contributions. Finally he made a down payment on enough lumber to roof the adobe walls of a church he was building himself. . . .

When I was nominated as a candidate to the state legislature, Spence volunteered to be my assistant campaign manager, and when I was elected, no one was more pleased than my friend Spence. He was also selected to go as a delegate to a convention in Santa Fe because he was a strong supporter of Judge Henry Kiker as a candidate for Governor.

Spence was a real booster of his community and was not ashamed that he had risen to a position of prominence and wide acquaintance in Clayton from the humble beginnings of slave parents. When Spence died, nearly all the businessmen closed their stores to attend the funeral. There were many relatives and out of town friends who were also present. Prominent political figures sent enough flowers to completely cover his casket, and he was laid to rest in the Sutton burial ground west of town.[7]

In Union County, Jack served as Justice of the Peace so long that he became known as the "Marrying Justice." Many couples named their first son after him, especially those unable to pay the required fee or to give anything else "in kind." In this duty he was aided by his faithful wife, who was anxious that things be done right for couples who were in too big a hurry or too financially pressed to arrange a more formal wedding. As her husband concluded the civil ceremony, Cordie Potter invariably offered an impromptu prayer for the health and happiness of the newlyweds.[8]

As a publicity stunt when the Marrying Justice was President of the Old Settlers' Picnic in Clayton one year, he offered to marry a couple "free" if someone would provide the license. It was reported that he had several takers to his offer.

Potter was of course a "joiner," and the organizations that he enjoyed the most were the trail driving groups whose main purpose was to gather together and reminisce, "perpetuating friendship and memories of those who 'went up the trail.' " He belonged to a number of such groups, and was the organizer and first President of the Trail Drivers of the Southwest. This later merged with another cowpuncher outfit, probably the Western Cowpunchers' Association which held its annual roundup at the Tri-State Fair in Amarillo each fall.

He also belonged to the Texas Trail Drivers and served both as First Vice-President and historian of this group.[9] Potter attended their reunions until he was well past eighty. He was also affiliated with the Old Time Cowboys' Association. In San Antonio in 1935, he joined in a request to the Texas Centennial Committee to erect a monument to the trail drivers on the grounds of the historic Alamo.

At the invitation of Governor John Miles in 1939, he met in Santa Fe with other interested old-timers to prepare for the Cuarto Centennial Celebration of Coronado's arrival in New Mexico in 1540.[10] Their purpose was to determine the exact location of early New Mexico Cattle Trails. From all accounts of the meeting, at which Potter was elected President, more time was spent in telling tall tales of the past than in locating old trails. President Jack's business sessions failed to arrange for a name for the group, and just before the meeting ended, he decided that the task should rightfully be assigned to the Governor![11] He enjoyed life and the company of congenial companions too much to be bothered with routine details, and he remained that way to the end of his days.

SEVEN

COWBOY AUTHOR
AND HIS FRIENDS

T rail driver Frank King once described Jack Potter as "the most cheerful liar west of the Mississippi."[1] He was speaking of "Upon the Trail in 1882," the humorous, rip-roaring account that Jack contributed to J. Marvin Hunter's book, *Trail Drivers of Texas*. J. Frank Dobie called this same story "the very best one in the whole collection of cowmen's adventures."[2]

No listener who personally heard them could ever label Potter's stories anything but the best. On the other hand, no reader of his original written versions would credit him with literary talent; without the generous assistance of both editors and friends his written stories would never have made the printed page. The story of Jack's career as an amateur author is as fascinating as his experiences on the trail.

True, Jack launched himself as a budding author by surprisingly winning a contest sponsored by the Pioneer State Tribune. This award for his early-day recollections provided the incentive he needed to engage in another type of activity after he sold Rancho Escondido and moved to Clayton in 1928. Thus encouraged, Potter began to send in accounts to the *Union County Leader*, copies of which D. H. Haley mailed on occasion to his cousin J. Evetts Haley in Canyon, Texas. "Doc" Haley, as he was known when he came to Clayton as assistant football coach in 1931, probably informed his kinsman that the writer of these stories had information that might help in the preparation of his current manuscript. Prior to this time, beginning in the summer of 1930, Potter and Haley had exchanged letters. Potter had supplied Haley with information on the Goodnight Trail for a book Haley was writing which was subsequently titled *Charles Goodnight, Cowman and Plainsman*.

Doc Haley's school office in Clayton was later the scene of several interviews with Potter which Haley recorded with a portable machine on small plastic records. At intervals Potter and Haley continued to exchange letters, Jack's usually being rambling accounts of trail days which Evetts carefully sifted for relevant details.

An interesting relationship developed between the writer Haley and the storyteller Potter. On November 18, 1932, Potter wrote Haley: "I was wanting to have a business talk with you and get you to take hold of my stuff and see if you could interest some publisher—the book business seemed to of felt the depression. I see a big cut in prices."[3] Evidently Potter had begun to send him many poorly typed and sometimes hand-scrawled stories of his recollections. Engaged as he was in the preparation of his own manuscript, Haley was not able to comply with this request. He wrote in reply on November 29, 1932:

Your letter, pertaining to your literary plans naturally pleases me very much. I appreciate the compliment, though wish to assure you that I only had in mind the matter of helping you out in writing the many stories that I have [received] pertaining to your reminiscences. Bugbee will be of help to you—I would not be able to improve your manuscript except to aid in its organization and the elaboration of certain subjects.[4]

The reference to Bugbee (Harold Bugbee, the noted Western illustrator) later encouraged Potter to contact the artist, as Potter's undated letter to Haley shows: "Bugbee got up a fine sketch for my Lew Wallace story. I have allready got the cut made, I believe it will be the first steer in a cut wearing five brands. I had the *Leader* editor put you on the subscription list. Are you getting it?"[5]

All during the next year Jack continued to send in stories to his hometown paper at the editor's request. He must have found editors elsewhere less indulgent, however. A letter to Haley dated December 27, 1933 indicates that he had received a little static on his "style and language.": "I'm sending you a copy of my Xmas story which won second prize in the Pioneer State Tribune contest a few years ago. I do believe that all editors and linotype fellers should be made to have an education in cowboy language and cowman history."[6] The cowboy language and spelling—or lack of it—and the erratically typed pages might have been a valid editorial complaint, but it was the readers' delight. Realizing this and being willing to undertake revision, the editors of the *Union County Leader*, Potter's hometown paper, urged him to turn in more accounts of early-day Clayton which they would run as publicity for a Western dance.[7]

Jack jotted down a few more stories and then stated that his supply of tall tales was exhausted. The enterprising editors, Franklin Vogt and Loy Cook, knew better, for they had heard too much about Jack Potter's early career to believe he would ever run out of recollections. They prodded him with leading questions: How many trail drives did you make? When you lived in Fort Sumner did you know Billy the Kid? How many lead steers did you have and what were their names?

The last question on lead steers fired Jack's memory. "Hell, yes," he replied, "I had a lead steer for each drive and I gave them all names. On my first drive, I used Randau; the second one was Bob Wright, named after my store keepin' friend in Dodge City; the third carried the name of Lew Wallace, after the former Territorial Governor. Then there was an old fightin' cuss I called Buck Shot Roberts, and the best one of all was John Chisum. My last steer was named Sid Boykin—he could smell water quicker than any critter on the plains."[8] Vogt and Cook knew they had struck a gold mine. "Keep writing, Jack," they wrote back. "Turn in your stories as rapidly as you can write them down. We'll polish them up for publication."[9]

For a while Jack hung around the *Leader* office regularly and he was quickly promoted—to "fightin' editor," that is! He took delight in talking to all office visitors and "bluffed out a feller or two" who had come to air grievances against the local editors. "When I was standing there with my big carcass blockin' the door, them boys in the back room became plumb sassy and brave," he said.[10]

The turbulent years of 1932–1934 were hard on all kinds of businesses, newspapers included. When Jack's editors gave up and a woman took their place, he also determined to quit his feature writing. He felt cowboy yarns would not fit in with the society, ladies' clubs, and bedtime stories that he felt the "petticoat editor" would begin to use. But the new editor, Laura Krehbiel, had two young lady assistants, and Jack was no match for their combined persistence. They made him a flattering offer of a weekly story, which would be compiled into a booklet on a fifty-fifty split.[11] Thus it was that the pamphlet *Cattle Trails of the Old West* was published in 1935. Within a comparatively short time the *Leader* had other editors. Jack was ready to quit again until the publisher, John Otto, put out a second collection of stories titled *Lead Steers*.[12] With two books on the market and a contract for continued weekly stories, Jack Potter found himself to be a full-fledged author.

During this time he had continued to correspond with Haley, who obliged him with editorial corrections, even sending in the finished manuscripts to editors himself in Potter's name.[13] Potter was also in correspondence with George Rainey, president of the Cherokee Strip Historical Society, who wrote on June 30, 1933, "I have read with much pleasure your contribution to the *Trail Drivers of Texas*, Ed. by J. Marvin Hunter. I am just completing a history of the Cherokee Strip, and I know it not out of place to insert one original story. Therefore please advise whether you personally have any objection to my using this story."[14] On the acceptance of Potter's story Haley wrote, "I see you are getting in demand as a historical author. I am glad you are contributing to the Oklahoma book."[15]

Haley had become acquainted with another writer of the western scene, J. Frank Dobie, whom Haley mentions in a letter to his Clayton friend: "Frank Dobie and I, while drinking a friendly glass of beer, decided that we should have you and Ab Blocker deliver one good lecture apiece to the students at the U of Tex. It wouldn't matter what you talked about, but you could certainly tell them some things they ought to know."[16]

Since Jack's stories "caught on" with New Mexico readers and his books sold out their first printing, he began to submit material to regional newspapers and western magazines. Quite a few times he repeated himself and told the same tale to several different editors, recreating the event with a sprinkling of exaggerated detail. He rarely varied the essential facts, however. For instance, the humorous account of his train trip back to the range from Cheyenne that was included in Marvin Hunter's *Trail Drivers of Texas* was retold under the title "Steppin' High" in his first book, *Cattle Trails*. The untrained cowboy author did not have much knowledge of copyrights or professional ethics in submitting material. But at any rate he never seemed to have incurred any trouble with his many editors, even in the case when on the same day, April 4, 1932, a story titled "Cattlemen in the Governor's Mansion" regaled the readers of the *Union County Leader* while an identical version titled "Cow and Sheep Governors" amused the readers of the Santa Fe *New Mexican*. Sometimes he even combined several published incidents under a new title.

An established western author of enviable reputation, S. Omar Barker of Las Vegas, New Mexico, became Potter's friend and helped to further his writing career. Interestingly, a recent letter from Mr. Barker to me reveals how this relationship came about:

The enclosed two letters and three magazine articles are all I can find in my packrat files concerning Jack Potter.

My editing and rewriting of Col. Potter's excellent material was at the request of the editor of *Ranch Romances* to whom he had submitted it. This was always entirely agreeable with Jack, and being the kind of man he was, he always offered to pay me for the help. But my part of the payment came direct from the publisher. Frankly, in those days the pay was not at a very high rate for either of us, but at least the dollar was still worth something then.

My writing collaboration with Jack must have all been in the 1930's and 40's. If my memory serves me, we worked together on quite a few other pieces for *Ranch Romances*, but I seem to have failed to keep track of them. Jack never offered the slightest complaint about any of the "fixing" that I did with his stuff. It was a most agreeable association.

Incidentally, his stuff was generally illustrated by the late Harold Bugbee of Clarendon, Texas. Whether Bugbee knew Jack personally, I do not know.

I'm afraid that's all the help I can give you on the old cowboy . . .

Mr. Barker also sent an original letter, dated April 10, 1947, which he had received from Jack Potter in which he discussed financial payment for the editing:

I have just received Check for twenty-five dollars for "lead Steer" and also a while back a Check for twenty dollars for "Pot Hook." Fanny said you done a fine job in doctoring both stories, and I'm very anxious to see them.

You send in your bill for work done and I will gladly send you a check.[17]

Potter also enjoyed an association with the noted historian and writer H. Bailey Carroll of the University of Texas. He wrote Carroll for his verification of the Fort Smith, Arkansas to Santa Fe trail. As Potter was considered an authority on the Texas and Northern trails, he was often "put on the spot," as he described it, by being challenged by later historians as to the routes of other early-day trails. Since Potter lived at Clayton in Rabbit Ear Mountain country, through which the Santa Fe Trail had passed, he had been asked why Josiah Gregg abandoned this portion of the regular trail in the late 1830s in favor of a route from Fort Smith to Santa Fe. Potter reasoned that Gregg outsmarted his competitors by shipping his wagons, goods, and teams down the Missouri River to Fort Smith. From that point he blazed a new trail and arrived in Santa Fe thirty days ahead of other traders. As any plainsman knew, grass on the southern route invariably greened up at least a month before forage on northern trails.

Potter was not able to supply his challenger with the exact route Gregg had followed, as there were no landmarks between the two Canadian River forks where Gregg was lost for a time. He therefore asked Professor Carroll for his version of Gregg's route to help settle the question and included his reply in a *Leader* article.

According to Carroll, who later traversed the route himself, Gregg must have traveled between the north Canadian and the south Canadian Rivers along the divide between the two streams. Gregg was pioneering the country and talking with strangers who did not use the same place names for the waterways. He could only describe what he saw. Since Gregg's journal referred to the North Fork, Carroll concluded that he meant *Wolf Creek* on the upper Texas Panhandle, not the Canadian River. Gregg was confused as to his location, and his conversation with a Mexican trail rider also added to his bewilderment. Because of the reddish tinge of the water, the Mexican called the Canadian River the *Colorado*. They were talking about two different streams. Gregg continued westward along a stream until he reached Tascosa in the western Panhandle, however, then went on to the Conchas Branch of New Mexico, to the Gallinas River, and thence to San Miguel and Santa Fe at last.

Carroll concluded by saying that Gregg's safe arrival in Santa Fe was a great accomplishment considering his ignorance of the country over which he traveled.[18]

Potter also had dealings with George Fitzpatrick, distinguished editor of *New Mexico Magazine* for quite a few years. Sometime in 1932 Jack wrote a long story for the *Union County Leader* titled "Capture of Geronimo and His Apaches." He began the story with a personal statement that "I was visiting at Old Fort Union, near Las Vegas, and read on a placard among the ruined buildings of the jail that 'Geronimo, Apache chief, and Billy the Kid were once incarcerated there.' "

Jack doubted the truth of that claim, even though George Fitzpatrick had mentioned the same story in his daily column in the *Albuquerque Tribune*, "Off the Beaten New Mexico Path."[19] Prompted by a vigorous argument among old-timers in the area, Fitzpatrick checked with the Information Bureau in Washington, D.C., and Potter triumphantly stated in his own article that "my version was verified," as no record could be found that Geronimo was ever taken to Fort Union. To add further weight to his position, Jack quoted a clipping sent him from an Indian fighter friend then living in San Antonio, Texas. The bulk of Jack's story gave an account of the famous chief's final capture and imprisonment.[20]

With his reputation as a reliable historian thus strengthened, Potter sent some of his stories to *New Mexico Magazine*. Quite a number of them were published, beginning with "Trail Dust" in 1935, and all had attractive illustrations by Wilfred Stedman, Santa Fe artist. Regarding the use of Jack's manuscripts in the state magazine, Fitzpatrick wrote to me on January 2, 1976, that

> As I recall, I had to edit all of his things—mostly a matter of straightening out sentences but also trying to retain the full flavor of his yarns.

Col. Potter and I became friends when I was writing OFF THE BEATEN PATH column in the *Tribune* in 1933 and 1934. I also used a number of columns about him personally.

One time I asked Colonel Potter where he got his title. He admitted he had just kind of picked it up. I got Governor Clyde Tingley to make him an honorary colonel, which took care of that.

Thus author Jack Potter officially became Colonel Jack Potter, and henceforth he signed all of his stories with the new title added to his name in abbreviated form—Col. Jack Potter. He was enormously proud of this distinction and saw to it that everyone addressed him properly. Between February 1935 and April 1949, while Fitzpatrick was editor, *New Mexico Magazine* carried ten stories by Col. Jack Potter on ranch and trail subjects.[21]

In a March, 1934 column Fitzpatrick carried a short story by Potter which began,

I never read "Off the Beaten Path" in the *Tribune* but my mind drifts back to the early eighties where if you expected to go anywhere you would pretty near have to be *off* the beaten path because there weren't many paths to be on.

On one such occasion I had orders to deliver a herd to the brand new town of Amarillo. I started from Stinking Springs as the crow would fly, bound for Amarillo. On the fourth day I arrived at the Texas line on the Frio draw where the XIT–Capital Syndicate owned a 200-mile front on the state line. The XIT foreman and a bunch of punchers came out and said they were stopping people from crossing the range, that they had designed two trails to Amarillo, one 50 miles to the north and the other 70 miles to the south.

I said "okeh," and they departed for the Escarbado Ranch. Just before it got dark I entered that XIT pasture through a gate, and it happened to be at the division fence between the Escarbado and Capital pastures—28 miles across to the eastern boundary.

Well, this was the first time in my life that I had a chance to measure distance that cattle could travel in one night. For my herd went that 28 miles. When daylight came next morning we were in sight of the east gate and went on out.

It gave me a great thrill to put one over on that XIT boss and his Montgomery Ward mail order cowboys.[22]

This story by Potter is not to be confused with the incident he related when he was turned back by the Goodnight people at gunpoint—a threat which he honored, but grumbled about in a number of stories written later.

Not only Jack Potter himself, but even his grandchildren were history conscious and knew their dates as well as the alphabet. In a column dated February, 1934, Fitzpatrick wrote that one of the grandsons challenged Potter on the date of Billy the Kid's death because his school history book stated the date was July *1878*. "No doubt most teachers know of this mistake in history," Potter was quoted as saying. "Why is this not corrected?

No doubt 50,000 school children have their New Mexico history learned wrong, and it will be hard to correct." The correct date of course was July 1881.[23]

While continuing his association with Fitzpatrick and *New Mexico Magazine* after 1935, Col. Jack also branched out to other publications, including the *Shamrock Oil and Gas, Western Live Stock, Hoofs and Horns, The Cattleman, New Mexico Livestock,* and perhaps others.

Eleven years before J. Frank Dobie met Jack "Yaqui" Potter in person, he had read Potter's incomparable account, "Up the Trail in 1882," which enlivened the pages of J. Marvin Hunter's book *The Trail Drivers of Texas,* published in 1920. Dobie's curiosity about the personality of a trail driver who related his experiences in authentic range-cowboy lingo was whetted by feature articles about Potter in the *Dallas News.* The opportunity for personal acquaintance came in October 1931 when Potter and twenty-seven trail drivers came in a bus to Vernon, Texas to dedicate a monument at Doan's Store on the Red River crossing of the Western Trail. Dobie so enthusiastically made the main address that one cowboy listener commented, according to Potter, "that old cowboy orator sure can holler." He did not know that Dobie always loosened his tie, pushed back his hat, and roared out words with a vigor equal to roping a calf.

It was at this meeting that Dobie became friends with Potter, and they spent long dark to daylight sessions in recollecting and exchanging trail stories. Dobie was delighted with his new friend and described him as a man "who summed up in himself the whole trail driver and range experience."[24]

An irregular correspondence between the two was carried on for a number of years. Potter's casual manner and characteristic speech showed up in an undated letter to Dobie, beginning "J. Pancho," and breezily calling him "Frank, you old jelly bean." Sometimes Potter would address his Texas University professor friend as "Dear old trail boss." Once, in an unusually short letter, Potter complained, "Your old drag driver, As you grow old you have almost forgot how to get up a real letter—it might be since the Volstead law has gone down in history, you can not get the old time tonic that builds up inspiration."

To build up Dobie's inspiration, Potter included a sketch of Beaver Smith's saloon at Fort Sumner and typed the caption "Where Jack Potter sowed his wild oats."

For several years the two men continued their friendship through correspondence and an occasional visit. Potter described one of the times in his hometown paper in this manner:

I was waiting at the bus terminal in Austin on my return from Pleasanton and Boerne when a fellow walked up and said, "Aren't you the same hombre that slipped by here last fall without stopping? Didn't

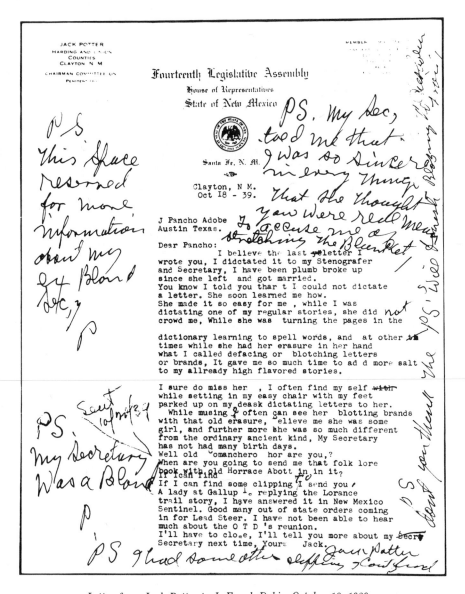

Letter from Jack Potter to J. Frank Dobie, October 18, 1939.

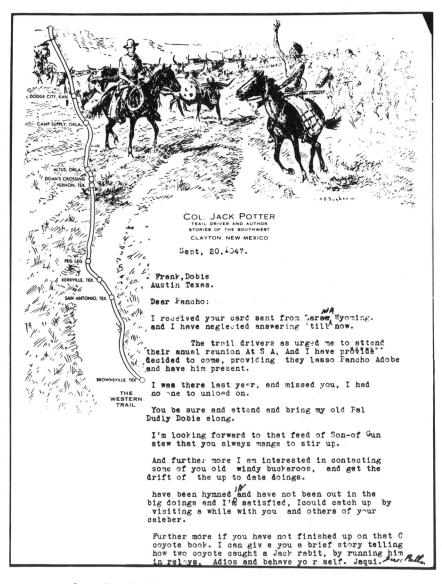

COL. JACK POTTER
TRAIL DRIVER AND AUTHOR
STORIES OF THE SOUTHWEST
CLAYTON, NEW MEXICO

Sept, 20, 1947.

Frank, Dobie
Austin Texas.

Dear Pancho:

I received your card sent from Larae, Wyoming. and I have neglected answering 'till now.

The trail drivers as urged me to attend their anuel reunion At S A, And I have provide decided to come, providing they lasso Pancho Adobe and have him present.

I was there last year, and missed you, I had no one to unload on.

You be sure and attend and bring my old Pal Dudly Dobie along.

I'm looking forward to that feed of Son-of Gun stew that you always mange to stir up.

And further more I am interested in contacting some of you old windy buckaroos, and get the drift of the up to date doings.

have been hymned and have not been out in the big doings and I'm satisfied, Icould catch up by visiting a while with you and others of your caleber.

Further more if you have not finished up on that C coyote book. I can giv e you a brief story telling how two coyote caught a Jack rabit, by running him in relays. Adios and behave yo r self. Jaqui.

Letter from Jack Potter to J. Frank Dobie, September 20, 1947.

you know Austin was the capital of the longhorns and all old trail drivers? With a gesture, he said "Vente" and I followed him to his automobile. "Entre" and I promptly got into the car. When we pulled up before a house he opened the door on my side with the word "Afuero" and then commanded "Passe." I went into his home and sat while he telephoned his friends saying, "I have an old ladino trail driver in captivity. Come on down and identify him." That was one grand time we all had that day.[25]

In 1939 Potter and the editor of the *Union County Leader* brought out another printing of the same material included in *Cattle Trails* that had first appeared in pamphlet form in 1935. Dobie wrote the preface for this volume, which was titled "Belling the Lead Steer." Concerning Potter's stories he commented, "I hope that old Yaqui's ebullient propensity for taking the bridle off, throwing the skillet away and letting the panther scream will not ever be curbed—Here is the stuff of history, it being understood that history is something more than naked literalness."

On Feb. 21, 1939 Jack wrote to Mrs. Dobie, mentioning that the *Leader* had commenced on *Lead Steer* in a slow way and complaining that those "eastern fellows couldn't understand cow language like he and J. Frank used." A few months later Jack wrote to Dobie himself: "Dear old trail boss: I have stampeded to you through the U.S. mail two 'Lead Steer's' and I hope Jim Farley's riders will round them up and corral them at your camp."[26] Farley's riders happened to be the postmen serving at that time under Postmaster General Jim Farley.

Dobie was away from Texas for some time, and Potter evidently missed his letters. He mildly complained when he was hospitalized with a severe foot infection that it had been so long since he had received a letter he "hardly knew what to write." Then in a characteristic way Potter described his hospital experience and the doctor's verdict of amputation of the offending member: "If that toe has to come off, let's call in some old open range waddy and have him to shoot it off, and give the matter a little color and publicity." He concluded the letter by telling how he spent the time keeping his typewriter company with stories he was writing for the *Star-Telegram* and *Amarillo News*.[27]

In one of the last letters to pass between the two friends, Potter wrote that he had studied over what "you said about telling the truth in a lying way." Then he vowed he would never tell another lie except at the regular reunion of the trail drivers, when it becomes necessary to "keep up my reputation."[28]

Although Potter reissued his stories over a period of years, by 1947 he was writing less, except for an occasional article in *The Cattleman* or the *New Mexico Stockman*, which published the last article in the Potter file after his death. In letter and conversation, however, Potter continued to speak of his hopes of publishing a third book of trail stories which he intended to call *Beyond the Pecos*. He was never physically or financially able to see this project through to completion himself, since he did not want to offer his work to an "eastern publisher" who did not appreciate cowboy lingo. Undoubtedly there would have been a ready market for such a book, and the manuscripts which he intended to include were, like most of his other work, first published in the *Union County Leader*.

Unlike trail rider Frank Collinson, a contemporary of his, Potter concentrated on the humor and horseplay which was characteristic of his age rather than on the details of cruelty and hardship of the buffalo range and cattle drives, which Collinson described in his book *Life in the Saddle*. Both men gave an authentic picture of life as they knew it, though Potter lived and wrote for about ten years after Collinson's death. Both had accurate memories for historic detail which gave an authoritative flavor to all their writings. Potter was much more prolific in his work, however, and contributed experiences of a much more varied career to the history of his period.

One of the WPA Writer's Project members said of Jack Potter after editing some of his material: "He describes his work among his daily companions and gives intimate glimpses into everyday life. He is a true son of the open spaces, straight-shooting and happy-go-lucky. In his stories are to be found the smell of gunpowder and sweating horses, the sound of thundering hoofbeats and the exploits of supermen of the prairie."[29]

Jack Potter himself was one of those supermen.

EIGHT

END OF THE TRAIL

When Jack Potter was no longer actively concerned with the Legislature and no pressing business occupied his time, he began to spend long hours at a popular gathering place in Clayton. On sunny days, the sidewalk benches in front of the Eklund Hotel, which was built in 1898, were filled with men whose memories of livelier days provided fodder for extended bull sessions. Political commentaries on the local, state, and national scene were also offered in such gathering places as the bar in Carl Eklund's hotel.

Carl Eklund—the Swede Kid—and Potter became staunch friends although there was a marked contrast in their appearance, background, and politics. Potter wrote in the *Union County Leader:* "He wore a derby; I wore a Stetson. He drank Hapstone Rye; I drank whatever I could get. He had toured the country on a train; I toured at 12 miles per day, herding a bunch of longhorns."[1]

Sometimes the group would sit around the big stove in the lobby, warming themselves as well as their recollections. A few shots of spirits from the bar sharpened their wits and loosened their tongues.

Of all the men who gathered there, no one held forth with such gusto as Jack Potter. His stories brought guffaws of laughter, respectful silence at mention of tragedies and killings, and general acceptance of the dates and events he quoted as being the gospel truth. In spite of his exaggerations, which he called "stretching the blanket" to make a good story better, he was usually credited with remarkable accuracy in recounting long past happenings.

He liked to tell how Senator S.W. Dorsey had changed the names of landmarks around the Clayton area.[2] After Dorsey had laid out his ranch, the Triangle Dot, from the ruts of the Santa Fe Trail, he used to travel this trail in his stagecoach over the plateau from Mt. Dora on west. As he viewed those mounds that loomed on the horizon which were apparently nameless, he began to call them after his relatives. Round Mound was changed to Sierra Clayton and later *Mount* Clayton for his son. Mount Dora was named for another relative, as was Mount Margarite. He did not change Rabbit Ears Mountain, however, which had been named for the Cheyenne chief, Orejas de Conojos.

In addition to his storytelling at the Eklund Hotel, Jack Potter enjoyed a social life with his wife in church and town affairs. Their home was always open to their friends and to their children's varied activities. Since they had lived in Union County for many years all the citizens knew Jack and Cordie Potter.

November 11, 1934 was a gala occasion for them. At that time a host of relatives and friends crowded the Methodist Church of Clayton to extend congratulations and good wishes on their fiftieth wedding anniversary. Selected friends gave musical numbers and laudatory tributes to each of them. Their daughters and granddaughters served an elaborately decorated cake to many old-timers and younger citizens of the community. Their gifts and flowers from well-wishers festooned many tables around the reception room. This golden anniversary observance was a fitting climax upon their return from a holiday trip to San Antonio where they had attended the Old Trail Drivers' Association gathering. This remained one of Jack's favorite organizations.

Ten years later the Potters observed their sixtieth anniversary, which was a smaller affair, held this time in the family home. The account for the hometown paper, written by Mrs. Potter herself, gave the details:

> The joyous occasion of our sixtieth wedding anniversary was celebrated at our home, Nov. 11, 1944 with many of our kinfolks, children and grandchildren present. A number of gifts were received and a beautiful three-tiered cake, brilliant with sixty white candles, was cut and served to our guests. Also chicken sandwiches and coffee, making us indeed a happy party and anniversary.[3]

It is not often that both husband and wife enjoy throughout their lifetimes the esteem of fellow townsfolk that was given to the Potters. Some criticism was directed at Jack, mostly during his term as a legislator, but this is a natural consequence of politics. No ill word was ever spoken of Cordie. She was loved by all. Six months prior to their sixty-fourth anniversary, Cordie Potter passed away after a brief illness, on June 20, 1948. Her obituary, printed in the *Union County Leader,* gave generous praise to her efforts to better the once lawless community where they first lived in Union County. It credited her with organizing a Sunday School at the Lone Wolf Saloon, a building that served as a combination meeting house, church, and school. She also organized a "literary society" which met Friday afternoons in the Lone Wolf building. Cordie Potter published and circulated a small handwritten bulletin called the "Cimarron Mirror" among members of this same society. People of her hometown genuinely mourned the passing of this little pioneer mother.[4]

Friends over the state wrote many letters to her husband. He acknowledged one from his friend Omar Barker of Las Vegas, saying "It was awfull nice in you writing that nice letter paying tribute to my dear wife. She thought a lot of You and Mrs. B, She was always hearing something nice from you. The latest was from Mrs. Nix of Santa Fe. And she got a great thrill out of the two poems about our court ship and &."[5]

After the death of Mrs. Potter, Jack wrote in a sad short letter to Frank Dobie that the "booklet adressed to Mr. and Mrs. Jack Potter" had been received. He concluded: "I doubt if you heard of it, but Mrs. P passed away last June, and I sure do miss her."[6]

The zest Jack Potter had always had for life seemed to pass to a noticeable extent with the death of Cordie, the little lady whom he had been too shy to propose to except by inference with remarks about his prize pony.

Col. Jack, more often referred to as Uncle Jack in his later years, remained in the modest family home after his wife's death. Never a man of more than average means, his needs were simple to supply. Ethel, who lived close by, tended to her father daily and the other children came to visit on occasion. Jack continued on his rounds about town, talking and reminiscing with the few cronies who still remained. He even married couples with the usual frequency up to three days before his death. He passed away quickly, just stopped breathing, on November 21, 1950. His favorite portrait of himself over a double column story on the front page of the *Leader* compared his passing with the breaking up of the fabled one hoss shay—a likely simile for this prototype of the old West.[7]

Jack and his father, the Fightin' Parson, had both contributed much to the development of unsettled country in both Texas and New Mexico. Potter County in the panhandle of Texas was named for his uncle Robert who lived in that area. Had he known of it, Jack would have been justly proud of the House Joint Resolution of the Twentieth New Mexico Legislature, 1951, which read:

BE IT RESOLVED BY THE LEGISLATURE OF THE STATE OF NEW MEXICO:

Colonel Jack Potter, member of the House of Representatives of the Legislature of New Mexico during the eleventh, twelfth and fourteenth sessions, departed this life, November 21, 1950 in the eighty fifth year of his life.

As a member of the Legislature he gave valuable service to his state in helping to pass laws of lasting benefit to our people, and

As a pioneer cattleman he contributed much to the development of the livestock industry of this and neighboring states, and

As an author he recorded in books, magazines and newspaper articles much of the pioneer history of the Southwest that otherwise would have remained unrecorded.

It is hereby resolved that the sympathy of the Legislature of the State of New Mexico is extended to his family, and

It is further resolved that this resolution be spread upon the journals of the Senate and House of Representatives; that the same be published with the Session Laws of 1951; and that a properly engrossed copy thereof be transmitted to his family.

At last Jack Potter had reached the end of his long, long trail.

COL.
JACK POTTER'S
BEST TALES

LEAD STEERS

I have talked and written about lead steers so much that some of my old cow range amigos call me Lead Steer Potter. They claim that when I get to heaven I'll like as not squat down on my hunkers and explain to old St. Peter that I might never have made it up that trail either if there hadn't been a good lead steer in the herd to guide me to water on some of the dry drives. My wife don't even deny my story that it was a lead steer that first called my attention to what a purty little lady on horseback she was!

Well, that's all right with me. I moved a good many longhorns over a heap of cattle trails, marked and unmarked, in my younger days, and there were mighty few times when the sense and sagacity of some old high-hipped steer out in the lead didn't help me to get the job done. I've had some purty fair cowhands poke fun at me for claiming that a man can savvy what a smart lead steer wants to tell him just as plain as if it was said in words. But a good many of them, like this hombre I'll call Ol' Trouble Maker, have finally had to acknowledge the truth. Old Charlie Goodnight, whose favorite lead steer, Old Blue, became famous all over the West, always agreed with me that a longhorn steer could be smarter than a man in natural knowledge.

On this trail drive from old Ft. Sumner across the Plains to Amarillo, I had several purty fair leaders in the herd, but the best one was an ol' wrinkle-horn that the boys called Mala Suerte. In Spanish this means Bad Luck. I don't know why they called him that unless on account of this steer's hard luck in getting gathered from the wild bunch and throwed into a herd bound for market.

I was managing a big cattle outfit with headquarters at Ft. Sumner early in 1888, when we learned that the Ft. Worth and Denver Railway out of Wichita Falls had finally connected with their extension south from Denver, and were soliciting the cattle trade for shipments to be loaded at several points along the line. Old Tascosa, Texas, had been considered the cowboy capital of the Southwest for so long that all us old cowpunchers were plumb shocked to hear that a brand new siding named Amarillo had been designated as the main big shipping point.

"How in the Sam Hill," we said, "can they expect to build up a shipping town out on the bald prairie where there ain't enough water to boil a jackrabbit in?"

Anyhow, Bill Howard and other boosters began to turn up out in the Pecos country, urging us to drive our stock to Amarillo. John Hill, Sr. also made a round of the cow camps trying to persuade cowmen to drive to Clayton, N.M., a station farther north on the same line, and incidentally the town that is now my home.

Hill brought along a five-gallon keg of high-powered whiskey for a persuader, and it had some effect, all right, whenever he met herds drifting north or northeast with no set destination—just looking for a market. Some of them old trail bosses that had been facing dust storms, eating alkali dust, and drinking that terrible Pecos water, seemed to find Hill's persuader mighty refreshing. Clayton caught about 30,000 head of those stocker cattle while Amarillo was first getting started.

In late October 1888, when the roundups were finished, I was named to take charge of a pool herd to be trailed to Amarillo. This herd was made up mostly of a lot of old cows, bulls, off colors, culls, and wild old steers that had evaded earlier roundups. One of the pool men that went along was this Ol' Trouble Breeder.

It was about 200 miles a little north of east across the plains from Ft. Sumner to Amarillo. Today the modern U.S. Highway 60 combined with 84 runs a purty direct route to Clovis, N.M., but at the time my pool herd set out, all drives to or from that part of the Panhandle had been detouring out of the way by Portales Springs and Spring Lake in order to get water.

I decided to break the ice by heading right out across the plains the way a crow would fly if he was darn fool enough to want to make such a trip. There was nothing on the Plains to mark the route for me, and I was handicapped by not being able to point my wagon tongue at the North Star, like I was used to on trails running north. Water was also going to be a problem, and if a norther hit us on those shelterless plains, I knew it could get plenty tough.

But I had a number of old outlaw steers in the herd, among which I felt sure there would be some natural leaders, so I felt purty safe. Well, at least I knew whichaway was east at sunrise, so I pointed my leaders a little to the left of it and set out.

"Quick as two or three of them old crinkle-horns ketch on which direction we're aiming to travel," I told the cowboys, "they will line out and lead us better than a compass. Look at that ol' Mala Suerte. See how steady he's got his ears cocked east?"

"We made the first long waterless stretch . . . without trouble,
though we had to make a one night drive."

Ol' Trouble Breeder looked at me, plumb disgusted. "With a boss that counts on followin' a bunch of damn dumb steers," he observed, "maybe we better have stayed where we were on the Pecos!"

We made the first long waterless stretch (sixty miles) from Taiban to the Rhea Brothers Ranch on Frio Draw without trouble, though we had to make a one night drive. We were still a mighty long ways from the water on Frio Draw when them lead steers let me know by an occasional sorter high weave of their heads and the confidence of their stride that they had smelled it and knew where to go.

I pointed this out to Ol' Trouble Breeder and asked him if he could smell water yet. He said no, and he doubted if them lead steers could either.

71

We drifted slow down Frio Draw to the Lower Mill just outside the XIT fence, resting the cattle and letting them fill up with good grass and water before entering the XIT for the twenty-eight mile drive across their pasture on a dry, flat plain without water. We figured to start on this stretch the next morning.

Late that afternoon a loud talking hombre who said his name was Jim Cook rode into camp with a batch of his mail order cowboys. He told me he was boss of the Escarbado Division of the XIT and also of the Capital Division just south of it that had not yet been stocked. He asked me who the hell I thought I was to figger on driving across XIT land at this point, and didn't I know the Company had designated only two trails across their pastures, one sixty miles to the south by Spring Lake, the other fifty miles north by Channing.

His tone and language were plumb insulting, but I managed to keep my temper hobbled and tell him my name was Jack Potter and that although I had heard the XIT had ordered them a batch of cowboys from Monkey Ward or Seahorse and Sawbuck, this was the first time I'd had a close look at any of 'em.

"I'm not aiming to mince words, Potter," he told me. "You'll have to detour your damn cattle to one of them other trails. It ain't nothing to me how long it takes you. And I'll ask you not to try any fresh stuff, for if you're found inside our pasture, I've got orders to take you and your crew and turn you over to the nearest sheriff. Furthermore, we'll be back in the morning to see that you obey those orders!"

I let him ride away without any more argument, but I had an idear in my head; and if the way he kept looking off east acrost the XIT fence meant anything, ol' Mala Suerte had about the same one. I told the cook to fix supper and have his outfit loaded. I had the wrangler bring in the remuda and told the boys to catch out their best horses for an all night drive.

Between sundown and dark, the herd, remuda, and chuck wagon entered the XIT along the division fence between the Escarbado and the Capital Divisions. Heading east down that fence, Mala Suerte and them other old lead steers marched along like a bunch of soldiers. We kept a lively gait all night and by sunup we were outside the XIT's east fence.

Now, I don't want you to think I'm a tenderfoot. They are the kind, to hear them tell it, that galloped their herds up the trail thirty or forty miles a day. And they always drove big herds. Actually, an average good day's drive was from twelve to fifteen miles. But in the cool of the night, in an emergency, a herd can be pushed twice as far without really hurting them. The way we slipped this herd across the XIT that night proved it, for in this case there was no guesswork about the distance. It was a measured twenty-eight miles across that pasture.

As we journeyed on eastward with no houses, fences, people, cow camps, windmills, or anything else in sight but just the wide open Llano Estacado, Ol' Trouble Breeder got to grouching considerable to the rest of the crew. "With a boss that don't know nothin' but to follow a bunch of damn ol' lead steers that oughta be in cans," he complained, "we're just as likely headed for Hell as Amarillo. If we don't run into some civilization purty soon and find out where we're at, I'm quittin' the drive!"

Two days later we still hadn't sighted any ranch or sign of settlement, but my lead steers were striding out free every day. Early that morning I went out to relieve the last guard, and while the herd was leaving the bed-ground, I saw Mala Suerte start off jumping stiff-legged, bellowing some and sniffing the air. I knew that language plenty good. I dropped back to the wagon, untied my bed, and got out my overshoes, my old ear-flap cap, and put on an extra shirt made outa a Navajo blanket and started the day's ride with them boys making big eyes at me.

"Look at him!" scoffed Ol' Trouble Breeder. "I'll be doggoned if he don't think them precious lead steers have given him a weather hint!"

Some of the old boys did laugh at me, and none of them got out any of their heavy clothes. Most of them even rode without their slickers, for the morning was bright and sunny without a cloud in sight. About midmorning, as we drifted the herd along, all at once low black clouds came rolling out of the northeast, and almost before you could holler *boo* it had begun to hail. This was followed by a cold pelting rain and sleet. Soon a cruel, spitting snowstorm was slanting into our faces, and all hands knew that a norther had really hit us. It tickled me to see those old boys, especially Ol' Trouble Breeder, already wet and cold, trailing back to the wagon after their slickers and heavy coats.

It was too stormy to stop and get dinner, so we traveled right on until, with expected good luck, about the middle of the afternoon the storm cleared up, the sun came out, and yonder ahead across the llano we could see the breaks of the Palo Duro. Neither Mala Suerte nor any of those longhorns in the lead had ever been in those parts before, but when they sighted them Palo Duro breaks their ears pricked up and they struck out straight for them.

In an hour's time we were slanting down into Palo Duro Creek where we could look across and see the cedar log cabin of the T-Anchor camp on the other slope. Then purty soon we intersected the deep worn tracks of the big cattle trail coming up from the south. A cowboy rode down from the T-Anchor camp to see who we were, as they were not used to herds coming in from the west. He didn't talk rough like the Escarbado boss on the XIT. "You're welcome to the Palo Duro," he said. "Make yourselves at home, and there's a good fenced horse trap up yonder where you can throw your herd for the night and all get some sleep."

That sure sounded mighty fine to us, and to add to our satisfaction, we could see the smoke of a railroad engine off yonder to the east and knew that one more day would put us in Amarillo.

After the cook had fixed up our stomachs in good order, the boys all seemed mighty cheerful around the fire. But I could see they had some sort of a "wolf" they wanted to turn loose. Finally Ol' Trouble Breeder unlatched his lips and let 'er go.

"I've ridden cow range for a good many years," he said, "and I thought I knew the cattle business. Well, you and them lead steers had me mighty uneasy on this drive, and I'm still puzzled to know how you savvy their language. But at least I'm gonna say right here and now that you've won out!"

"Well, it ain't chaps and a big Stetson hat that makes a cowhand," I said, "though I expect Charlie Goodnight and myself are about the only trail bosses willing to admit that they can learn something from a good lead steer."

However, right here, I'll have to admit my own self that on one occasion, at least, I reckon I must have completely misunderstood a mighty smart steer. One foggy morning in Kansas I let my herd graze across a furrow line that was supposed to mark the boundary of the cattle trail beyond which cattle were not allowed to graze on homesteaders' land. When the fog cleared, I found myself right in front of a settler's dugout. An ancient, grizzly, chin-whiskered, scrawny-looking nester began to cuss me out purty mean. Right then I saw my old lead steer beginning to beller and paw up the earth.

Naturally I thought he was advising me to tie into the nester. But after I had given him a good punch, I got handed the biggest whipping I ever got in my life. I guess that old steer really meant that I should lay off that old battling nester if I didn't want to get took, and good at that!

TWO

CASE CLOSED

T he threads of this story reach across fifty years, from the dust of a trail herd in 1885 to the brief case of Federal Agent Alex Street in 1935—and back. In July of the latter year I happened to run into Alex, and though we were old friends, I was a little surprised when he said, quite seriously, "Jack, I've been looking for you. Come up to my room."

Street had been a frontier detective for some time and had the reputation of being able to look a man straight in the face and make him cough up his past.

"Alex," I said, when we had gone upstairs, "what the Sam Hill do you want with me? You know I'm one Texan that never held up no overland stagecoach."

"Didn't, eh? Where were you on the 8th of July, 1885?"

Well, that was fifty years ago, but it didn't faze me any. "On July 8th, 1885," I told him, "I camped with a herd not far south of the Arkansas River. Four hundred thousand head of Texas cattle went up the trail that year—and I had charge of the lead herd, belonging to the New England Livestock Company, headed for Ogallala, Nebraska. But we'd been thrown off our route by Kansas quarantine, onto the so-called National Trail up along the Colorado line to Trail City. And . . ."

"In your camp that afternoon," Alex interrupted, "was a fugitive from

75

the law that we were laying for—an hombre named Ted Arnold, alias Jim Underwood. But the next day, when you camped on the banks of the river, he was missing, and also the next day too. When you left Trail City we figgered this fugitive had circled around to dodge us, and would come join you again farther along. But he didn't. Remember a fellow coming into your camp looking for a job as a cowboy? That was an officer, looking for Arnold."

"You've sure got it right," I told him. "I knew that feller sure wasn't no cowboy by the way he handled his plate and the delicate way he sidled up to the chuck. But what's all this got to do with me holdin' up a stagecoach?"

Alex kinda grinned. "Never mind that stagecoach you never robbed, Jack. What I want to know is—just what became of this man called Arnold?"

"What difference does it make?" I countered. "That's fifty years ago. He'd be a harmless old man by now."

Alex had a prompt comeback to that. "We never stop looking for fugitives with a record, Jack, as long as they are alive."

So I told him that here was one, at least, that they would never catch—Ted Arnold, alias Jim Underwood, sometimes called Old Snake. And then I told him why. That is the other thread to this story.

With thousands of cattle to move, competent trail hands weren't any too plentiful. If a man looked like he'd make a hand, most trail bosses didn't inquire too close into his past before hiring him. Consequently most of the crews on those drives harbored a few fugitives drifting north to greener lands. Such a one was Arnold, whom we all knew as Jim Underwood. Not only a bad hombre, but quarrelsome and a bully. Underwood and a couple of others who sided with him as pals, caused me right smart of trouble on that drive. I held it down the best I could and put up with them because I had a herd to deliver.

Underwood actually laid plans for one of his scrubs to kill some of us (in our sleep) who hadn't backed down before his bullying. What made Old Snake's presence in the crew the hardest to put up with was the way he bullied the kid who was the horse wrangler. From Ogallala, this boy aimed to go on East somewheres to college. His name was Cox, but he was so curly-headed, girlish looking and timid acting that we called him Little Lord Fauntleroy.

He put up with Jim Underwood's bullying the best he could. Maybe I oughta have herded Underwood off of him more than I did, but a trail boss always had plenty to do besides nursing the wrangler. On this drive in particular I was kept plenty busy laying out a course and speed of travel that wouldn't throw us too close to other herds on the trail. You get too many herds close together and some stormy night a stampede will mix them and then there's Hell to unravel.

It didn't put any slack in my duties, either, when at MacKenzie Flat Crossing on the South Canadian, one of my last year's drag drivers showed up in a livery rig, all dolled up like a Kansas shorthorn, to inform us that Kansas had clamped down in earnest with their quarantine against Texas tick fever, so that to get through to Nebraska we would have to blaze a new western trail up through the northern tier of Texas counties to the Kansas line at Point of Rocks, thence to follow the National Trail north just inside the Colorado line. No matter how sorry I felt for him, with a new trail to scout I just couldn't spare time to look after Lord Fauntleroy. On the trail a man—or boy—looks after himself.

At the crossing of the Beaver, our fighting bully matched himself with a trail cutter who jerked his pistol out of his hand and gave him about the most terrible whipping a man ever had. Naturally black eyes didn't improve his temper any, and he took a heap of it out on the kid wrangler.

The feud kinda came to a head over a pair of cut hobbles. In the remuda we had a little bunch of ponies that seemed to be pals, and 'most every morning they would be missing. Their leader was a pony in our badman's mount. One night I told Fauntleroy to hobble a few of the main strayers. No sooner had he finished hobbling the little leader that was in Underwood's mount than that bad hombre walked out and cut the hobbles to the tune of a good cursing for the innocent wrangler.

Next morning this leader pony was missing as usual with a number of the other horses. "You're so damned smart, Jim," I told Underwood, "you can go hunt up those missing horses and overtake us later, but not too much later, for I will need all hands to get through those sandhills."

Toward noon, when we'd already got the herd through the sandhills, Underwood still hadn't showed up. As I rode back to see about the remuda and chuck wagon, suddenly the air was peppered with the sound of six quick shots. I put spurs to my horse and lit out at a gallop toward where I thought they'd come from. I couldn't work up any other thought but that our bully, catching Fauntleroy so far from the herd, had up and murdered him.

On reaching the spot, however, I was surprised to see Underwood's mount, saddle empty and the rider nowhere in sight. Fauntleroy was changing his own saddle to his own private mount, crying and blubbering like a baby. "Boss," he said, "that scrub came in and started cursing me and slapping my face. I've emptied my gun into him like I shoulda done long ago. Yonder he lays. I've got some pay coming—let me have whatever you can spare in cash. I'm goin' to overtake the herd, kill Snake's two pals, then pull out west!!"

"No," I answered, plenty stern, "you aren't going to do anything of the kind. You wasn't meant to ride no outlaw trail, and I don't aim to let you do it. Underwood sure had it coming to him."

77

*". . . suddenly the air was peppered with the sound of six quick shots.
I put spurs to my horse and lit out . . ."*

"But those pals of his—they'll kill me when they find out!" he exclaimed.
"That is, if I don't kill them first!"

"Maybe they won't find out," I said. "Let's get our heads to working.
The cook's a good half-mile behind. Unsaddle Underwood's horse, quick,
and bunch the remuda around his body and his saddle so the cook won't
take no notice. And don't be no jelly bean! Stop that cryin' and put on a
bold front when the wagon gets here."

Pretty soon here came the wagon rattling along, the team sweating,
the cook cursing. "Damn National Trail sandhills!" he shouted. "Hell's full
of such!" He was too mad from sand trouble with that heavy chuck wagon
to pay any attention to anything else—luckily for us. While he stayed
perched up on the seat in front, letting the team blow, I told Fauntleroy to
draw us some drinking water from the barrel, and while he was doing it, I

unstrapped the spade from the rear of the chuck box and let it drop in the sand. Then I told the cook to roll on, we would overtake him.

Quick as he was gone, we dug a long hole, rolled Underwood's corpse, saddle, and rigging into it and covered it as smoothly as we could. "This is one grave that'll have to do without a headstone," I told Fauntleroy. "Get your rope down and make out like you're going to rope the horses so they'll trample all over this place and make it look natural—for you see that dust back yonder? That's Noah Ellis with the next herd. You go on with the remuda and I'll hang back here and see that Noah nor his boys don't suspect nothing. The way I look at it, you've done a good day's work and all I ask of you is not to go into camp and start anything new."

In spite of his curls, the way he looked at me showed him up right smart of a man. "Boss," he said, "I know you're a friend of mine and I'm going to do whatever you say."

If trouble over this came up in camp I had made up my mind to finish the job by killing the first man that batted an eye at me. "You leave it to me to explain to the cook about that spade. Don't you let on as if anything out of the way has happened."

With that parting advice, I rode slowly back to meet Noah Ellis's herd. The situation still looked sorta touchy to me in case some of Noah's boys got to reading sign.* I rode along with the pointers, visiting with them, hurrawing them some, as was cowboy's custom. My object was to see that they would pass that fresh filled grave without noticing.

We were within about a hundred yards of it when the lead cattle suddenly broke into a trot, heading straight for the spot. There they commenced bawling and pawing up the ground like cattle do when they smell blood. I tell you, it had me scared till my heart was bobbing around right back of my tongue.

"Them steers smell blood," said one of Noah's hands, "and cattle never lie. What you reckon's been goin' on here?"

Before I could think up a good answer, another one of the point riders saved me the trouble.

"Somebody's beefed a calf and buried the hide around here somewhere," he said, riding in to push the leaders on as if it were a matter of no concern to him.

I dropped back to the flank and visited back and forth along the herd till the drags come up and passed on, then hung back for the remuda and chuck wagon as well. When they had all passed safely, I begun to draw easier breaths. "Jack," I said to myself, "it seems like last spring since you left camp this morning. You'd better be getting back!"

---

*A cowboy expression for evidence along the trail.

First thing I did when I got to the wagon, I gave the cook a good bawling out for not strapping that spade on good and tight that morning. He was in too bad a humor over this sandhill trail to remember how he had strapped it on. I reckon I had some kind of a reasonable surmise figgered out to give in regards to what may have become of our fighting bully, but I never had to use it. Because the first mention made of him was by one of his pals.

"Old Snake, he musta gone back to the Beaver to kill that feller that whipped him," he said, and everybody seemed to agree with him. Later, as the herd rolled on northwards, one or another was heard to remark that it looked like maybe Old Snake had come off second in his settlement with that trail cutter back at the Beaver crossing, but that was all.

Nothing more was ever said between Fauntleroy and me. He came to me privately and offered to stand guard, since he was the one responsible for us being one hand short, and I let him do it. Curly locks and all, for a mere kid he proved himself right smart of a man when it come to the pinch.

So instead of a fugitive killer, whipping a long-tailed pony west, maybe to ride the outlaw trail for life, Lord Fauntleroy could now go on East to college as he had planned when the herd was delivered, and I never have suffered a single regret about my part in it.

Fifty years later, almost to a day, I watched Federal Agent Alex Street write in his memo book as follows: Case No— United States vs. Ted Arnold, alias Jim Underwood, for train robbery. Case closed by proof of death by affidavit of Jack Potter.

THREE

POT HOOK JOHNSON

O ne afternoon way back in the 1880s, we were camped with the wagon on the outskirts of Ft. Sumner when we spied a lone rider dusting down toward us on the old Portales road. Lone riders were nothing strange on the range in those days, but we were right smart excited to figure out who this one might be. This old Portales trail was what you might call the gateway from the Texas Panhandle and eastern New Mexico plains to the Pecos country, and over it at one time or another traveled just about every noted character, good or bad, who ever ranged in the whole Pecos area. Billy the Kid had traveled it, as had John W. Poe and Sheriff Pat Garrett, who tied the last knot in the Kid's tail in 1881. We figured this rider might be some well-known hombre like them or like Charley Siringo, the Pinkerton's range detective, or Barney Mason, or the Sanctified Texan. No telling who might ride down the trail.

But when he reached the wagon he turned out to be, apparently, just another feller split up the middle with a horse between his legs, and a fairly easy tongue in his head.

"Howdy, folk," he greeted us. "My name's Happy Johnson, and I expect I'll have to stay the night with you and maybe longer. I've got a tired horse, I'm out of chuck and finances, and I've either got to ride a chuckline some place, snag me a job, or starve to death."

I didn't offer him a job, but just told him to throw off his saddle and make himself familiar with the coffeepot. Next morning after we had caught our mounts, one of the boys laced his saddle on what looked like a purty mean bronc, but was mightly slow about mounting him. After our visitor had watched him stalling around a while he said, "If you're scared to climb on that bronc, I'll top him for you for half a dollar."

"You've made you a deal," said the cowboy.

Happy Johnson promptly mounted the bronc and thumbed him in the neck. I never saw a horse buck harder, but our volunteer peeler stuck on top of him like a leech. When he had got the bronc quieted down, had dismounted, I told him I hated to see a man who could ride like that roaming around with the strays. The best I could offer him was a temporary job as cook, since the cooksie we had was itching to resign anyhow.

I don't recollect that I asked him much about whether he could cook or not. In those days 'most any cowhand could wrangle up a chuck wagon meal if he had to, and I had no doubt the boys would put up with him till he got more practice—that is, if he warn't too long learning.

It turned out that I had put our stomachs in mighty good care. Happy Johnson—he later got the nickname "Pot Hook"—wasn't long in becoming famed as one of the best sourdough cooks that ever boiled beans in the hard water of the Pecos country. In fact, this was the beginning of a career that for a few years had no equal. But it was not all at the tail board of a chuck wagon by any means. For four bits Johnson was always ready to top off a rough bronc for any cowhand in camp, and he was also fond of gambling and dealing monte. What sure 'nough put the salt in his career, however, was his practice of dragging a big loop.

There was no law in those days to keep an ambitious fellow from branding mavericks on the Public Domain, just so he didn't get caught putting his iron on any that were not weaned from their mothers. Many a cowboy built up a good herd for himself that way. Nevertheless, the big cow outfits objected to such a practice, and considered the mavericker as no better than a thief. But Johnson started dragging his big loop anyhow, and as far as I know, was the only chuck wagon cook ever to start a maverick brand in a big way.

One winter I was ordered to take the wagon and a small crew and start what we called a floating outfit to drift over the range and brand up what calves we could find that had been missed on the fall roundup. My orders were to move in on the river and establish a bog camp* when we got the floating job done. That was when various riders began telling me about noticing a new maverick brand on the range. I'd suspected Johnson

---

*A camp on the river in a damp spot.

and the horse wrangler were up to something besides playing marbles when away from camp, but I never could catch them.

When time came for the spring roundup of the big range lying between Ft. Sumner and Seven Rivers, I started down the Pecos with a full crew to work the west side. A spring rain had filled a good many water holes out on the prairie and started some grass to rising, so there were always thin cattle moving out away from the river. In these bunches there were still a good many dogies and mavericks.

Upon moving the wagon from Huggins Arroyo to make noon camp at the Bosque Grande, we riders ahead of the wagon found ourselves waiting dinnerless several hours for a chuck wagon that didn't show up. So after while I rode back to find out what ailed our cook. About four miles out I found the wagon with one horse taken out. Off across the prairie I saw cattle bunched up, the smoke of a fire, and two men on horseback. I rode over to them. It was Johnson and the horse wrangler just finishing a branding job. They had turned their roundup loose, but I rode around through the cattle and found seven head with the Pot Hook brand still a-smokin'.

"Well, Johnson," I said, "from now on I reckon your name is Pot Hook. I knew 'most every cowhand was mavericking, but I didn't think a range cook would have the gall. There's a hungry bunch of boys down the road waitin' for you to feed 'em."

"Now, Boss," he said, "you've made your spiel. Take this from me. A cook's got to drive a team and get up three meals a day, rain or shine, with water so hard it rattles the beans. Besides, you never fail to camp me on the side of the Pecos where the sand blows the worst, so you can't blame a feller for branding a few mavericks on the side to better his condition. Am I fired—yes or no?"

"No," I said, grinning at his concern. "I reckon any cook that can get up sourdough like you can has always got a job!"

So Pot Hook Johnson kept on mavericking whenever he had the chance. I think it was the second fall after that that the cattle business got purty dull, and I had to cut my winter crew down about half, which didn't leave Pot Hook so many to cook for. Ft. Sumner and the Plaza Nueva, just off the military reservation, were only about a mile from camp, and Pot Hook put in purt' near full time there.

He had got mighty unpopular with the cattle companies, and orders were out to a good many line camps not even to feed him if he showed up there. But at Ft. Sumner he had him a big time a-gamblin', peddlin' marihuana, bootleggin', dancin', and often just breedin' trouble between the Spanish-American population and the Anglos. Even after he lost his whole herd of Pot Hook cattle in a poker game, he never missed a *baile,* and he was said to have got up a purty serious love affair with a Mexican girl named Dolores Sanchez, daughter of old Madril Sanchez.

But *Gancho,* as the Mexicans called Pot Hook, had one habit the people didn't like. After dancing most of the night, he'd go to a corral and "borrow" a burro to ride home, turning it loose after he got back to our camp. The Mexican people complained about this, so one night after a big wedding dance for some old Don's daughter, I decided to frame him. I knew he was tired and would be stealing a burro to ride home after the baile was over. I also figured he was getting to be too big a nuisance around there, and maybe this would be a good way to scare him into quitting the country without anybody getting hurt.

I got several Mexicans to lay in wait and catch him on the road riding one of their burros, then call me to interpret for them, as Pot Hook couldn't savvy much Spanish. Sure 'nough, they arrested Gancho for stealing one of old Pascual's burros and sent a messenger to camp after me. When I got there they had Pot Hook staked out and hobbled.

I acted plumb unconcerned and asked what was the matter. All Pot Hook answered was "Plenty," but them Mexicans cut loose with lots of words and gestures, all in Spanish, of course.

"Pot Hook," I said, "I hate to tell you, but they've decided to take you up to the Bosque at sunup and hang you as an undesirable citizen and burro thief."

"Boss," said Pot Hook, "can't you use your influence for a compromise?"

I told him I would try and held some more consultation in Spanish. I reported to Pot Hook that they sure 'nough had their necks bowed to hang him. Then I also told him in a low voice that his only chance to escape was to flank a willow tail horse west—both mighty quick and far.

"I've got fifteen dollars," he told me "and ol' Shack Simmons owes me twenty. You git me a plug pony and see if you can frame up some way for me to escape, and I'll sure do my best to ride out of it—even if it does leave you short a cook."

"I'll find another cook," I assured him, "but you can't find another neck. You just set tight. They won't hang you till sunup anyway, and meantime I'll rustle you a horse."

Of course these Mexican people were all my amigos, and along toward sunup I didn't have any trouble sending them off for a cup of coffee, leaving just me and one guard with Pot Hook. I had got an ol' plug pony saddled up for him just around the corner of the adobe barracks buildings. But some of the men I'd talked to while getting the pony had told me, "Hell, you can't trust Pot Hook to ride very far, because the first son of a gun he runs into that looks like he might be interested in a game of monte will find himself dealing a few with Pot Hook."

So we decided to give him a send-off calculated to keep him headed straight west. I sent several vaqueros up to the crossing of the Pecos to hide under the banks with rifles and six-shooters.

I managed to talk the guard into trusting Pot Hook in my custody, but just as I was ready to give him the word to take off, the doggone booger tried to balk his way out.

"Look, Boss," he argued, "couldn't you sorter postpone this here escape till I can fix it up for Dolores to pull out with me?"

"You stay here many more minutes," I told him, "and all the romance you'll ever experience will be a solo dance at the end of a rope! Get going now!"

"Well, anyhow," answered Pot Hook, "I sure ain't goin' to head straight west. I've heard about that hundred mile stretch. I ain't goin' run into it like a scared rabbit. I'm aimin' to bend off by Zuber's Ranch on the Yeso and pick up some refreshments."

I told him to suit himself about that, but to get going—and he sure got. He dodged around the old barracks walls like a prairie chicken, flapped himself onto that pony and kicked him out fast. By the time he got to the Pecos crossing he didn't seem to be much worried, for he had slowed down and was singin'.

That was when those vaqueros I had hid out under the river banks opened up with their fireworks. To say that he made that ol' plug pony run like a shot-at coyote might be exaggerating, but he sure took a fresh start—straight west, this time.

In about ten days I had a letter from him saying that he had been doggone lucky to get away at all, because a whole damn posse had fired on him from ambush at the crossing and chased him for miles.

"You remember me telling you," the letter said in closing, "that I was aimin' to detour by Zuber's Ranch? Well, Boss, I just didn't have the time! Adios."

FOUR

THE
JINGLE-BOB
HERD

The jingle-bob used by John Chisum to identify his cattle was the most distinctive mark of ownership in the West. Chisum's cattle were cut out of the roundups by the earmark instead of the Long Rail brand since no one but Chisum had such a mark. They got to calling him "Jingle-Bob Chisum," and his men were known as the "jingle-bob peelers."

The making of the earmark has puzzled most people, even the best of cowmen. You have pretty near got to see it on the animal to understand it. I have seen many descriptions of the jingle-bob, most of them wrong. One writer described it as a long slit in the ear. Another claimed it was a strip of hide skinned off the shoulder and allowed to hang down. Dean T. U. Taylor, author of *Chisholm Trail and Other Routes*, describes it as a double dewlap on the brisket. And the most unique one of all, a tenderfoot writer, says it was a piece of tin, folded with a note in it that showed the color of eyes, hair, date of birth, and ownership—the tin being attached to the ear with a piece of wire.

Once while attending the Trail Drivers' Reunion at San Antonio, I was telling about the earmark. We got to arguing about how it was made. All of them had different ideas, and we didn't seem to be getting anywhere. Finally one of the group said, "I want to see how it is made. Come, get in my car and we'll go to the slaughter house and have Potter show us." I showed them and convinced them at last.

They held a veal calf while I started in on the earmark. I said, "Fellows, this is very simple." I stuck my knife in the lower part of the ear next to the head, allowing about one-fourth of an inch for the bob to swing on and then cut upward to the top of the ear, bringing my knife out on the upper half of the ear. This left two-thirds of the ear to drop down, resembling earrings on a lady. John Chisum was very particular about having the earmark made just right. He would take his knife in hand and show the boys how *not* to make the upper slope too long. This was done to prevent defacing of the brand by cutting off the bobs. The upper part of the ear was left so short there was not enough left to cut on.

Chisum ranched in Denton County, Texas before he came to New Mexico in 1866. Fayette Tankersly, his neighbor in the Concho country, told me that Chisum used the same jingle-bob brand on his ranch there.

In June 1866 Charles Goodnight and Oliver Loving, enroute to Fort Sumner with a large herd of cattle for delivery to the Fort to relieve the food shortage among the Navajos, stopped in the Concho Valley.

The drive to Fort Sumner interested Chisum and his neighbor, and they were eager to learn more about reports of great unstocked cattle ranges west of the Pecos River in New Mexico.

When Goodnight returned to the Concho, Chisum questioned him and made up his mind to go on an inspection tour himself. Instead of going alone, he decided to round up 600 head of his oldest and largest steers to drive along on the chance of selling them to the commander at Fort Sumner. In the fall of 1866 he arrived at Bosque Grande, fifty miles down the Pecos River from Fort Sumner, and there established a camp that later became his permanent ranch.

Chisum found Fort Sumner well supplied with beef but was advised that his beef steers could be used by early spring. While herding his steers, he made plans for establishing his main ranch there and surveyed enough range to accommodate one hundred thousand head of cattle. The only menace was the Indians.

In the spring of 1867 he commenced moving his jingle-bobs from the Concho Ranch to the new Bosque Grande Ranch. For several years he held down a hundred mile square of grass land. His only neighbors were the Casey family on the Hondo and L.B. Maxwell of Fort Sumner. He expected to continue furnishing beef to the commander at the Fort and was quite disappointed when in the spring of 1868, before the spring drive of cattle had arrived, orders came that the U.S. Indian Department had decided to send the Navajos back to their old home at the Shiprock Agency and Chaco Canyon. Nevertheless, Chisum got other contracts from Fort Stanton,

Fort Union, and Fort Thomas, Arizona. For ten more years he continued to hold his big range intact.

He often told his niece Sally Chisum, known as the "queen of the jingle-bobs," that he was going to get married and settle down when his herd increased to the one hundred thousand mark! According to a story told at the roundups, he pretty near made a proposal to the widow of his attorney, Alexander McSween, who was killed in the Lincoln County War. A year after the cattle war ended, Chisum made up his mind to remunerate the widow of McSween for work her husband had done for him during the days of turbulence. He gathered up two hundred very choice heifer yearlings to present to her.

I asked Mrs. Sally Chisum Robert if she could verify the rumor that her Uncle John was in love with Mrs. McSween. "Well," she replied, "there could be some truth to that story. You know that Mrs. McSween was a beautiful, educated lady, a musician who had been raised in proper society."

"It took just such a person as Mrs. McSween to attract the attention of Uncle John," she went on. "I can remember when Uncle John selected those yearlings out of his large herd. There was not an off-color or scrub in the whole bunch. He started them to Lincoln or a place nearby which was five days' travel away. About the time the cattle were supposed to arrive at their destination, Uncle John dolled up in his best clothes, his shop-made boots, his calfskin and Stetson hat and lit out himself for Lincoln. I was informed later that Uncle John had delivered the herd at the mouth of the Ruidoso and was riding along with Mrs. McSween, giving her the benefit of his knowledge of raising cattle. I was told that she asked for permission to use the jingle-bob earmark on the increase."

"Well, let me think," he mused and rode along quietly for a short while. "Not unless you will give me the promise that some time in the near future we might merge our herds and you will become queen of the jingle-bobs."

Sally Robert continued her story. "Before she could answer, a puncher galloped up on a horse wet with sweat and told Uncle John that he was on the trail of stolen stock, the trail leading toward the Mescalero Indian Reservation. Uncle John wheeled his horse and started off in quick pursuit without saying a farewell word to her. To my knowledge, he and Mrs. McSween never met again. About the same time, in the year 1879, his cattle empire began to crumble. Uncle John was supposed to own and had on the range, sixty thousand head of stock cattle. He had sold ten thousand head of cows to Wiley and Scroggins and thirty thousand head of young cattle to Hunter and Evans."

I asked her if there was any truth to the story that Chisum was broke and had to liquidate or that he had sold out, lock, stock, and barrel, to Hunter and Evans.

"The thirty thousand head that went to Hunter and Evans was just a little more than one year's increase," she told me. "It was always calculated that the calf increase, if branded up well, would equal one half of the cattle on the range. The relationship between Uncle John and the Hunter–Evans Company was never strained, regardless of the rumor. The Lincoln County cattle war was a hard jolt for Uncle John and took a big toll on his interests. Cattle rustlers began to increase their herds with jingle-bob mavericks. Then in the early 1880s drought cattle from Texas commenced arriving by the thousands. The worst menace of all were the nester cowmen. They looked like nesters, brought their families, but to my knowledge they were expert cowmen in disguise. They prospered and built up large herds."

About that time I asked her about the jingle-bob mark and why Chisum was so particular about it. She gave me a clear enough answer. "It was because, if the mark was cut right, it was impossible to change it and leave enough of the ear to make it look like anything. The U brand up on the shoulder was hard to deface also. You know that Uncle John back in 1875 abandoned the Long Rail brand as he thought it was too big. After that he used the U high up on the left shoulder.

"The cattle rustler was badly handicapped in defacing the brand and earmark both. The only chance was to find an animal poorly marked or branded. When thousands of calves are branded one right after the other, lots of times mistakes were made by placing the U brand upside down. With a little fixing, this could be made into a round-top A. Other brands were made up to cover up such mistakes on the U brand. Sometimes if the U were placed upside down, there was also an ox-yoke brand which could be made out of it."

I was sure glad to have this conversation with Sally Chisum Robert and have her set things right for a bunch of tenderfeet cowmen who would believe anything they heard.

FIVE

DRAGGING A
BIG LOOP

W hen a Yank named Sam Maverick started in the cattle business in Texas, he asked his neighbors why they burned those large brands on the flanks of cattle. They explained it was an identification mark so each man could recognize and claim his own animals.

"Well," Maverick said, "If that's the case, I can recognize my cattle from my neighbor's by not branding mine."

The only trouble was that in a few years he found he had about the same number of cows he had started with. The cowboys, whenever they found an unbranded yearling, had been putting their own brands on. They laughed and said, "It's just another one of Maverick's bunch."

That way the name stuck for all unbranded calves that had been weaned from their mamas. Many a fine herd and personal fortune has been built by branding maverick calves. The greatest paradise for this type of young cattle was on the Pecos back in the 1880s when all but the river front was public domain. A maverick was considered free to all if its ownership couldn't be traced. Some of the cattle companies claimed the mavericks by owning the water holes where they watered, but some of these same companies would discharge their punchers if it became known that they were dragging a big loop.

One spring a meeting was called by the cattle companies in Roswell to plan the roundup, and a ruling was agreed upon, designating each man's range where he could claim and brand mavericks for himself. It was ruled that the boys who had grown cattle on the range could not be barred from branding mavericks, but that fresh yearlings not running with grown cattle would be claimed as mavericks and held in roundup herd until the owner could prove he was entitled to them.

There was a bunch of Texas nesters on the Penasco, all smooth operating cowmen, and at the CA cleanup, those nesters commenced claiming their share of the drove of mavericks that Buck Powell, range roundup boss, had brought in. One old feller, riding a swayback mare, first cut out a pair of work oxen and then commenced adding to his cut with yearlings. When he finished he had about thirty head. Buck Powell rode out to him and explained the ruling made by the cattle companies. He asked the feller if he had proof that he had grown cattle on the range.

"Hell, yes," the nester replied. "Can't you see my yoke of oxen there?"

Buck looked at the work oxen and gave a big grin. "You have a fine yoke of *steers*, rather prolific, I'd say. I'll have to take this matter up with Jim Hinkle, our manager. I'm satisfied he'd be real interested in buying this particular pair of steers."

"Just tell him they're not for sale," replied the nester crossly as he rode away.

There was another incident that concerned a feller name Tex, an industrious but ignorant old boy who learned his ABC's by applying brands on cattle. Tex had a lot of stories about the great roundups on the Conchos and the exploits of the cowboys who operated around there. We all got tired of listening as we had made several drives over the Texas trails ourselves. I myself thought that I knew the cattle business from A to Z.

One day I started in behind what I thought was a bull maverick that looked to be a yearling or some over. I circled for a few hundred yards, then roped and tied him. I got my iron in the fire, and while I was waiting for it to get hot, Tex came up on the run. He jumped off his horse, ran on by me and grabbed the yearling by the head. While I was trying to figger what it was all about, he bent his nose down close to the calf's mouth. Without a word, he went to the fire, pulled out the iron, then untied the animal.

I thought he was acting plumb loco. "Tex," I asked, "what the Sam Hill is the matter with you?"

"This here yearling has a mama," he snapped at me, "and he's been with her just this morning."

"Why, how do you know that?" I asked.

"Because his breath smells plumb milky, that's why," he said. "You claim to be a cowman, but you couldn't even get a job wrangling horses down on the Conchos where I come from."

Well, our relationship was somewhat strained after that. We went back to camp where we had supper and turned in. I couldn't sleep, thinking of my humiliation, and I shook Tex awake and said, "Listen, it's bad enough for a cowman to have an ignoramus like you to try to teach him something about cattle. What's more, think of the value of that big yearling you made us lose."

"Huh," he grunted, "a ten-year-old ought to know when a maverick *is a maverick*. I'll show you tomorrow. Bull yearling's just like a boy leaving home. If he gets into trouble, he'll go back and hunt up his ma."

Sure enough, next morning, there was our supposed maverick, nursing his mother along with all the other calves in the pen.

ROUNDUP COURT

Back in the open range days you seldom ever saw a newspaper, being isolated in cow camps and on roundups. Our only chance of getting news from the outside world was from transients passing through, or some of our own boys coming from town. But frequently we didn't know what to believe, because the country had such a bunch of cheerful liars. People going, coming, and visiting these cow camps formed the habit of what they called "loading a feller up."

Many a puncher played the goat in spreading news he had heard that was not authentic. To cure the boys of this lowdown habit, the roundups all over the cow country from the Pecos to the Cimarron organized range kangaroo courts to try and cure those smart alecks who were spreading false reports. When anyone told anything that did not sound authentic, he had to offer positive proof. Then, if the yarn still seemed shady, he would be tried before the "range jury" who assessed a punishment to the guilty of six strokes with a pair of leather chaps. When a feller had to double his length over a bedroll to assume the correct position, those chaps could be pretty mean punishment.

I believe the first puncher tried on the northern roundup was Len Mansker. He had a great personality and could look a group in the eye and tell them a tall tale and make it stick. It was after the terrible blizzard of

October 1889, when thousands of cattle drifted away from the herders and left many a trail hand or roundup boy stranded out on the prairie without shelter. About the third day of the storm, Len Mansker arrived at Clayton where many of the boys had found their way into shelter. Most of them were telling tales of their endurance, but then Len came in with a real thriller. He and his pardner, he said, had followed the herds at night until they reached a canyon with plenty of timber and a bluff on the north side which gave protection from the wind. When they were busy building a fire, Len's horse, Old Dorsey, fell over, stiff as a board, plumb frozen stiff.

"Well, we camped there two nights and a day and finally got so hungry we had to decide whether we would starve to death or turn savage and eat the horse." Len admitted, "We cut a loin off, broiled it over the fire and ate it without salt."

The second day they walked to the Foster ranch, got shelter, and borrowed a horse to ride double to town. This story soon spread over the country and the daily papers at Denver related the story of the cowboy who was forced to eat meat from his frozen mount. It was generally believed —until next spring, that is.

In the general roundup at the upper Pinovetes Arroyo, Old Dorsey turned up, alive and fat! It also happened that Len was in this same roundup and he was sure surprised to see that old horse. At noon that same day he was asked to show cause why he should not be tried in kangaroo court for misrepresenting the truth. Papers for his arrest were prepared with the warrant reading:

ROUNDUP ASSOCIATION
vs.
Len Mansker

Well, now, he was found guilty, given the punishment of six strokes with the chaps in roundup court and also in the town of Clayton. Len Mansker was an awful poor loser, and he claimed that this roundup had more professional liars than he was. "I want to first mention Captain Foster," he said, "who was trying to get home to the ranch from that high country around Mount Dora. He stopped at a claim shack along in the night to rest and get warm. He lit a match and saw that a fellow was sleeping in the bunk. Since he did not want to disturb him, he lit a fire, pulled off his boots, and warmed his feet for a while. When he was good and sleepy, he pulled back the tarp and found that the feller was plumb dead."

Len continued, "I now want papers got up for Captain Foster himself. I want to charge him of telling a tale about a dead man in his bed and he never brought a finger or toe back to prove his story."

Captain Foster, the old roundup boss, came forward promptly, ready for trial. He said, "I'll plead guilty, but only to a part of this, and I'll offer reasons why I did not bring anything along to prove what I had seen. When I pulled that tarp back and saw that the man was dead, and *grinning* at me beside, I figured I didn't have any time to collect a souvenir of proof."

"Did you take time to put your boots back on?" he was asked.

"Hell, yes, I couldn't buck them snowdrifts barefoot."

The verdict of the court was soon brought in: Not Guilty!

Case number two was then called:

ROUNDUP ASSOCIATION
vs.
Jack Potter

"Charged with misrepresentation and seeing too much, contributing to the delinquency of cowboy youths by learning them how to tell tall ones, misrepresenting the talent of his many lead steers, quoting too much about Lead Steer John Chisum and the great blizzard."

I was immediately placed on trial on the charges quoted above. I was first asked if I really had a lead steer named John Chisum and why I had let him have his way when I was supposed to be escorting the herd myself in that blizzard, when I was supposed to be finding the way to I. L. Ranch on the Tramperos.

"Well," I answered, "it was humiliatin' enough to me to have to give in to Old John. When we intersected that trail out on the prairie that leads down to the Pedernal and on to Tascosa eighty miles to the next ranch, we came into this trail at an angle and I had made up my mind to follow it. Old John, he just balked and kept on going in the direction he had selected for himself. I rode up to him and gave him a big cussin' out and told him if he had more sense than me to just go right ahead and I would follow him. Besides that, I told him how wet, hungry, and tired we were, horses included. If we didn't find shelter before night when the snow melted, a bunch of hungry cowboy corpses would be discovered out on the lone prairie. Chisum kept on going and led us straight to the brakes on the Tramperos and the ranch where we found everything we needed, corrals, food, shelter for both man and horse."

The judge of the court said, "You have sure related a wonderful story, but what proof have you got?"

I mused a minute and told them that Chisum had drifted away in the blizzard after we had arrived at Clayton and that I had gathered him on this roundup, that I could produce him as proof when the herd came to water. So I got a few hours grace until I could put a fast one over them by showing them a *different* steer.

When the herd arrived at camp I got on my horse and cut out a big old rangy longhorn, drove him up and told the group, "Here is John Chisum, take a look, he's my old lead steer."

The trial was called into session again, and I was certainly expecting a quick acquittal. Len Mansker came on the stand again and swore that the steer I produced was not John Chisum at all, that this steer I had brought up had been on the same range for five years and was known to all as a stray.

Well, I was sure stunned. I couldn't deny it and was pronounced *guilty* with an extra penalty for misrepresenting a harmless old lead steer who couldn't defend himself. Orders were given to stretch me over a roundup bed with my face down and to give me six strokes with the chaps, not only that day, but to continue the same punishment for six extra days.

All I can say is that after this incident, all of us were a little more particular about the tales we told, even an old cowboy who was celebrating in the usual manner and told a real wild one in the Mansker saloon. He came running in one night shouting that twenty or thirty hobos had been thrown off the train that had just pulled up to the station.

"I thought," replied one of the bystanders, "that you knew that any such wild tale as that had to be backed up with proof."

Without another word the old boy rode off toward the station, fired some shots, and came back in just a few minutes herding them hoboes into the saloon. He told the barkeeper to give them each a full glass of whiskey, called the restaurant man to prepare a meal, and then marched them old boys out to the pond and made them wash up good and proper. Then he sat them down at the tables and asked, "Is this sufficient proof?"

It turned out that these hobos were riding East, all on one freight, going to look for work, and none of us there that night could deny that the old cowboy had really offered us proof.

It was quite some time before the veteran punchers could cure their habit of exaggeration, but it didn't take them long to change their tune when someone would mention the ROUNDUP COURT.

T H A T
O R N E R I E S T
S T E E R

Buck Shot Roberts, the orneriest steer of them all, got his name from an old fellow who was killed at Blazer's Mill down in Lincoln County after matching shot for shot with a bunch of deputies, Billy the Kid included. After what happened there, all other names suggested for the steer, such as Billy the Kid and Pat Garrett, seemed plumb mild.

I first met up with this critter in 1887 when wintering with another cowhand at a dugout camp at Mora Springs, forty miles southwest of Fort Sumner. A bunch of mavericks got to congregating around the dugout and bellowing so loud they got to be an all-fired nuisance. Since there was no law against branding weaned stuff, I decided then and there to start a maverick brand myself. After roping and tying down a half dozen, I found one more, a sure nuff big yearling which I burned with my brand. He was not much trouble until I untied his legs. He just lay there with a mean look in his eyes, making no effort to get up. So I hit him over the back with my rope and he came to life—pronto. Showing plenty of bravado, he first charged my horse, running him off and leaving me afoot. Then he knocked me down flat. When I got up and tried to run to my horse, he beat me there and knocked me down again. Then I reversed myself with several yards' head start, but he gained on me, breathing that old hot breath right on my neck. He knocked me down the third time and I decided I had had enough. I lay on my stomach like a dead man, hoping he would leave. No such luck. He got astraddle of me and started pawing up dirt all over me. I don't know how long I lay there, but finally I peeked up to see him looking off to the west at a bunch of burros and sheep that had come in to the water hole. He quit pestering me and charged them instead. The sheepherder began to yell for help, but I had had enough of that fight and left—pronto and for good.

This animal, after that day when I branded him, was missed in the roundups for two years. Then on the east side of El Capitan Mountain at Agua Azul, an isolated place in the hills, we rounded him up again. As we met each other face-to-face, he gave me that same old fierce look. He was fat and sleek by then, but his wild gaze was the same as it was two years back.

"Why, you ornery old devil," I cussed, "if it wasn't that I have contracted to sell you for $20, I'd shoot you between the eyes right now. But needing dinero, I'm willing to let bygones be bygones. I'm going to try to get along with you after all."

When we finished the roundup and took the trail, who should lead out but this ornery old Buckshot. Everything went well until the trail herd got to Canyon de Agua early one morning. It was a community toll road at that time, and the herd had to be stopped while the trail crew argued about the toll. As we did not come to an agreement after some little discussion, my lead cattle got restless and started up the road. Finally a bunch of these hombres walked into the herd to stop them. But a few of the cattle started back, with old Buck in the lead, brushing through that crowd of toll collectors, knocking them down purty darn fast. So we compromised on the toll without any more talk and the herd went on through.

At Las Vegas stockyards Buck ran over a brakeman and had full charge around the railyard for a while. He must have had a couple more fights on the way because at Oren Junction he was unloaded with the seat of some overalls on his horns. On the bill of sale a notation was scribbled: "Beware, vicious steer in this shipment."

These cattle were contracted to the Bloom Cattle Company to be delivered at Las Vegas, shipped to Oren Junction, Wyoming, then trailed to the Milk River Ranch at Malte, Montana, away up by the Canadian border on the Northern Railway. It was customary to hold the steers there for at least two years to mature. After quite some time I read in a paper where a vicious steer in transit at a St. Paul siding had broken a car and was at large until a policeman shot him. I knew it must have been old Buck. I allus figured that he would wind up in big trouble and die "with his boots on."

EIGHT

KILLING THE
LOBO WOLF

Back in the early days of the open range a tenderfoot walked up to Uncle Billy Follice, a range boss for fifty years, to ask how long it would take a feller to learn the cow business.

Uncle Billy scratched the ground with the toe of his boot a minute before he replied. "Son, most any one can learn how to rope and ride in a few months. This means strength and muscle but not brains. But to learn the cow business a person must—why, why, you never quit learning."

And Uncle Billy was right. To learn the cow business a person must learn how to class the different ages of cattle, how to care for them on the way to market, and how to keep them gaining flesh while on the trail. The cowman must also know how to cook, to butcher, and how to shoe his mount, fight prairie fires, or raise up an old cow if she's down in a weakened condition. And before he's finished with his cow education, he must know how to trap or otherwise snare that wiliest of all prairie animals, the lobo wolf.

In the early 1890s when the wolves in our part of the country were particularly destructive, cowboys had definite orders to use every effort to run down and catch wolves if they saw any of them ornery critters. I believe the greatest wolf hunter at the time was "Wolf-Hound Tanner." He kept a string of fast horses and a string of common old hounds to follow the trail. Tanner would also use an extra man to lead the change of horses while he ran the wolves. Another interesting wolf killer was Jack Callis. He hunted in a different manner from Tanner by following roundups and putting out bait.

Probably the prettiest catch I ever saw was in 1894 after we had made our roundup on the Cienega with Buck Miller in charge. He pointed out a big steer to Callis and told him to take him up the arroyo and shoot him behind the shoulders. Callis did this but took care to inject strychnine into the veins before the animal died. The next morning after starting out on our circle up the trail at the edge of Rabbit Ear Mesa, we found six lobos, all dead from chewing on that poisoned steer. They seemed about the same size and age so they must have all been from the same spring litter. I suppose the mother wolf must have been off hunting because it is very seldom that a mature wolf will taste dead meat or allow its young to do so.

Another incident in my own experiences that comes to mind was one that happened back early in the 1890's at Fort Sumner on the Pecos. We had just finished our spring roundup when we got orders to take two crews to the Tu-les, a watering place on the edge of the plains, and to hunt out them four-legged bandits of the range. It was the time of year that pups would be leaving their lairs. Our orders were to put in twenty days destroying pups and shooting the old ones if we had a chance. Two posses of ten men each were sent out to a camp near a spring and an old adobe house. The posse I was leading rode through the sand hills for seven miles until we came to a hardpan flat surrounded by gypsum bluffs several feet high. We soon found a lair, dug into it with pick and shovel, and pulled out seven pups. We killed them all and kept the scalps as there was a small bounty on them. After scouting around for an hour or two longer we found the second lair. Here we unearthed five more pups. These were almost old enough to leave the lair and no doubt had received a few lessons of the wild from their mother. We killed four of them and one of the boys kept the runt for a pet. He tied a piece of worn halter around its neck and carried the pup on the pommel of the saddle.

When we got back to camp before dark, he tied this here pup to a stake in the old adobe house with a pan of water and some fresh beef near it. The pup refused to eat or drink though we knew he was hungry and thirsty. As we were setting around the fire that night a wolf came to the top of a sandhill not more than two hundred yards away and set up a pitiful howling. She kept it up all night and none of us could sleep much.

The next morning fresh water and beef were offered the pup but again he refused to touch it. When the second night came, he still had not tasted either food or drink. We thought he would just starve himself to death. At dark while we set around the campfire that mother wolf started up her wild howling again and kept it up, growing louder and more desperate by the minute. After listening for a while longer that tender-hearted old cowboy got a rope and stake pin and went after the pup. He took him out about seventy-five yards from the camp and picketed him. He told us, "I'm going to let him nurse his mother and stop that howling." In a minute we noticed that the howling had stopped and the feller went back out to check. He found the rope had been gnawed in two pieces, and the pup had vanished with his mother. That wily old wolf had outgeneraled us all and released her pup to hunt with her again.

THE
SANCTIFIED
TEXAN

One of the most picturesque characters of the Old West was the "Sanctified Texan." His history was cloudy and the only thing definitely known of his past was a rumor that he was a fugitive from a southern state. His last place of residence was in the Adobe Walls country where he had been killing buffalo, up to the time the herds were wiped out. He was Hugh Leeper.

But no matter how shady his past may have been, it was generally conceded that he was fairly well educated and was an accomplished scholar of the Bible. At least he quoted it a lot. Later he achieved real fame in the Pecos region as a prophet of sorts. Many a hazardous adventure of the early seventies was started upon assurance by the Texan that things would go all right, that "their time had not come."

After Billy the Kid made his sudden demise without even firing a shot by taking the chances that he did the night of the tragedy, people believed in the Sanctified Texan with a stronger faith than ever. They were sure that "Billy's time had just rolled around." Leeper's next prophecy was that the old saloon on the banks of the Pecos would be the next to go.

Shortly after The Kid's death, the Maxwell estate was sold to four large cattle companies. This included the Fort Sumner headquarters building then used as a ranch home, a store, dance hall, and one side of the reservation which started a new plaza on the south. Called Maxwell for a time, this second Fort Sumner lasted for many years until the Santa Fe Railway built through and the station was located five miles north of the old fort, marking the third site.

It made the Sanctified Texan very happy when the manager of the cattle companies gave orders for old Beaver Smith and his associates to move on. "The saloon," he said, "is a curse of civilization, a place where desperados meet, drink vile whiskey, and settle their disputes under the smoke of their forty-fives." After Smith had left, the Texan prophesied that the building itself would also be destroyed because of its evil associations that made it a disgrace to posterity.

The adobe saloon building was on the west side of the main officers' quarters about two hundred feet out between the building itself and the Pecos River. Shortly after the cattle companies had taken over the property, the river began making a short turn towards the old Fort and often in a swift current forty or fifty feet of the bank would cave off in one day.

Finally the manager became alarmed and feared that if the river continued its rampage, the old fort itself would be in danger. He let a contract to build a channel on the extreme west side of the bend and thus to straighten the river channel and deflect the current to the west side. When the work was finished, the Texan just laughed at the manager's efforts and claimed that it was "of no use because the river channel could not be changed. It will take the old saloon with it."

He was sure right that time. The first rise in the river filled the newly cut canal with red sand and the current began to slop at the west bank. The river rose for thirty-six hours. One afternoon, when everyone was watching the high waters and feeling mighty uneasy, they heard a loud, thundering noise and saw water splashing high toward the sky. When the water lowered, the saloon was gone, and the Texan had again prophesied correctly. The next morning the water continued to run fast right through the canal and cut a permanent straight channel. All that was left of the old saloon site was a muddy sand bar. Leeper's reputation increased till he had everyone believing that he could really foretell the future. Not that they were superstitious or anything like that. "It was the Lord's will."

One night some time after this during a hot poker game, Barney Mason was losing quite a stack. He had bet his money, his horse and saddle, and had finally got down to his boots and hat. The players around the table thought that he would surely quit and were quite surprised when Barney pulled off his coat, sold it for two dollars, and called for the same amount in chips.

The feller who bought Barney's coat looked into the pockets and found descriptions and pictures of fugitives from other states which Barney, as undercover man for Sheriff Pat Garrett, was carrying around with him. One of the descriptions fitted the Sanctified Texan exactly. Since the new owner happened to be a friend of Leeper's, he took him aside and showed him the picture of himself as a wanted man.

That old Bible-quoting feller took the news real calm like. He turned to his friend and said, "Well, just tell the folks that *my time has come* to move on. I'll be seeing them when the Roll is Called Up Yonder. Adios!"

TEN

THE INDIAN SCARE

I can remember the spring of 1887 at Old Fort Sumner on the Pecos, when several chuck wagons and a large crew of men had assembled to commence work on the general spring roundup. While sitting around the chuck wagon, we saw a lone rider coming in from the southwest. Within a few minutes he galloped up to camp with his mount lathered in sweat. He kinda choked up when he told us that "Indians were coming!"

"How many?" we asked, just to see what he would say.

He answered in a shaking voice, "At least a million or more!"

Now this feller was called Pecos Breezy, a line rider who was known to be excitable and had such a big eye, he always exaggerated on the numbers. The boys commenced poking fun, saying that they had heard too many big lies from him to believe this story.

We kept on kidding him: "Who the hell ever heard of Indians being in this country at this late date? You should be tried in our roundup court and show proof of what you have told us." (The roundup court was the cowboys' way of dealing with big windies and administered a punishment of six lashes with leather chaps to every man found guilty of exaggeration.)

The scared man had a fast comeback and said, "I have no time. The proof is on its way now. As for me, I'm changing mounts and plan to leave this here premises pronto. Sabe?"

He seemed so serious that the boys began to halfway believe him. Across the divide between Fort Sumner and Yeso Creek we could see the dust a-rising. One of the boys claimed it was just a trail herd coming over the Goodnight–Loving Trail. Another said that at least six miles of dust was spreading over the trail. The most conservative old boy of the bunch muttered, "We better get our guns ready, for there's something unusual in the air."

After a while we could see several riders coming down the slope. A government escort leading half a dozen Indians soon galloped up. They told us that the Government man had charge of several hundred Jicarillo Apaches and was moving them from their reservation near Fort Stanton to the San Juan country of northwest New Mexico. He asked for permission to camp on the Fort Sumner reservation. In less than half an hour the lead Indians began arriving, and they kept riding up for more than an hour. Each Indian family was driving its livestock. Then we had to believe at least a part of Breezy's story. But the boys were peeved for being "taken in" and got out a warrant for Old Breezy and brought him to the roundup court for misrepresenting the number of Indians. They said he claimed there was a *million or more*, and they thought there were only about *five hundred*. Well, they found him guilty of misrepresentation alright by about nine hundred and ninety-nine thousand and five hundred. So it wasn't long until Old Breezy was bending over to receive his lashes with leather chaps.

There was one man who told a "big windy" and got away with it. Here's the way it happened. There was a smallpox epidemic raging in northern New Mexico and old Horseshoe Curly and his two pals had come down with the fever. They were sent out a mile from town to an abandoned claim shack that was used as a pest house. With a small supply of provisions, a gallon of whiskey, and old Santa Cruz Hidalgo and his woman for a nurse, they suffered out the disease. In about thirty days they were released, a scabby looking bunch if you ever saw one.

Well, Old Curly lit out for the spring roundup, but he had been wised up about the prairie court and he knew he would have to have some kind of proof if he told he had survived the smallpox with no doctor and no medicine. He went to John Spring's butcher shop that usually kept fish in stock, and bought a fish, scraped a few scales into a matchbox which he stowed away in his pocket.

When he arrived at the roundup, of course the boys crowded round to hear him tell of spending four weeks in the pest house. One of them spoke up and demanded proof.

"Hell, yes, I can prove that I had smallpox. Just look at this box of scabs that I done saved for you."

With that those fellers really scattered, hollering as they ran, "We'll take your word, just throw that darn evidence in the fire and clear away from here."

ELEVEN

TRAGEDIES ON THE PORTALES ROAD

T he early cattle history of the Pecos River and Fort Sumner area of New Mexico often mentioned the Portales Road, which served as a gateway to that section. Many hunters came to the Portales Spring to kill buffalo and antelope for their winter's supply of meat. Often such men as old Ramon Silva and the Celedon and Trujillo brothers of Fort Sumner also went there to hunt mustangs for their horse ranch.

The flowing Portales Spring was located under a ledge of rock which made a deep overhang, thus forming a porch or *portal*. This was the only shelter of any kind for many miles around and it also furnished an abundant supply of water for wild game.

In the past someone had erected a rock wall on the south side of the portal, probably for protection against Indians. With the solid earth bank on the north and the caliche rock fence on the south, defenders could hold off an enemy for days, since their water supply was dependable.

I believe the first white man to locate at Portales Spring settled there in 1878, a buffalo hunter from the Yellow House Canyon country by the name of Doak Good. He was then employed on the Star Mail route to Fort Sumner from Singer's Store near present-day Lubbock. This was a fraudulent daily mail route swindle which had been framed by a group of smart politicians, including Senator S. W. Dorsey of Arkansas. These men later were accused of accepting pay for a daily route over this sparsely inhabited country though some of the post offices received only monthly service, and many none at all.

During Doak Good's stay with the mail route he made Portales once a month and finally selected this location for a ranch. He started with a small herd, lived there until 1887, by which time his herd had increased to at least a thousand head. For the first four or five years, Good lived like a hermit, but later built a two-room adobe house with a shingle roof, the only one in that part of the country.

I will always remember the first time I saw Doak Good, as I had heard much about this old buffalo hunter. After a hard ride down the Portales Road from Fort Sumner, I stopped at his ranch, hoping to spend the night. When I hollered out to get his attention, a fine looking *young* man blue-eyed, nicely dressed and intelligent looking, came out to answer me.

"Is Old Doak Good around? I want to stay the night with him. My mount is tired and so am I."

"Light and unsaddle," he answered. "I'll take care of your horse. I'm that feller, Old Doak Good you're looking for."

I was sure surprised and was glad that I had made his acquaintance. That night he told me about how Billy the Kid and his gang had used Portales Spring as a rendevous. He didn't say whether they came or went in his absence or if they had his permission to stay. I was afraid to ask.

He also told me about trouble he was having with a neighboring stockman named Jim Newman who was located at Big Salt Lake. He knew that sooner or later there would be trouble over water, as Portales Spring had the best stock water and more of it. When he built his house he wisely left a low loft for sleeping quarters between the ceiling and roof. This provided him with a hiding place and also a lookout through a small window at each end. One morning as he was dressing, he saw a stranger whom he suspected was a hired gunman. The man kept sticking his head around the corner of the shed, then drawing back. Good felt he was waiting for a chance to shoot. He got his trusty buffalo Sharps rifle, went downstairs, and stood at the corner of his adobe. The next time the man peeped around, Good took careful aim and shot him.

After this killing, Good was afraid to stay there by himself. He picked up a transient kid, just about fourteen years old, called Portales Bill. He was a queer looking feller with long shaggy hair that stuck up through his old crownless hat. I remember him as the toughest and bravest kid I ever met.

Good sent him over to the Newman roundup to cut out some yearlings which Good thought belonged to his herd. The roundup boss disputed his claim and was surprised when the kid didn't back down but even threatened to take them under the smoke of his .45. This kid later became the terror of the Staked Plains.

Cattle rustling became quite a menace in the late 1880s, and the large syndicate XIT set out to put an end to it with an organized posse of about sixty men. They rounded up a bunch of stolen cattle with defaced brands at Mesa Redondo near Tucumcari, New Mexico, and in the process several rustlers were wounded.

A little later Eugene Logan, Texas Association Inspector, with eight men surrounded Portales Bill, Doak Good's friend, in a shack at the Franciso de Baca ranch near Endee. Logan hollered out to him, "Bill, come out. Give up your gun and surrender. You're surrounded!"

Portales Bill answered with a shotgun blast and a stream of profanity. "I'll never surrender to you sons of bitches, not me!"

One volley from the posse put the quietus on his bravado, and he died as game as he lived. Later, a member of the coroner's jury told me his real name was William MacElhaney and that he was just a transient kid up and down the Portales Road.

There was another killing involving a young man near Limpierado Creek (water hole with rock bottom) on the old Portales Road. It seemed that a mature cowman by the name of Al Johnson was beating up a kid wrangler called Wiley Rainbolt. They were struggling and rolling on the ground when the kid spied a gun half hidden under the covers of a roundup bed. He managed to grab the gun, and shoot his assailant, killing him instantly. He ran for his horse, saddled up and was ready to escape down the Portales Road when the trail boss stopped him. "You're foolish to run," he advised, after Wiley had explained the circumstances. "You just acted in self defense. Go on back to Fort Sumner, you won't be arrested. I'll vouch for you." The kid was glad to do as the boss said and returned to his job as wrangler.

Another time four young men rode down toward Portales, looking for work. When they had camped for the night, they began to quarrel and all drew on the one who started the fracas. He was shot and the other three scattered pronto. I later heard that two found work back in Fort Sumner and the third went on to Tascosa where he assumed a new name, and in time became very wealthy in both cattle and land. When he moved on, I think he took his own name back and continued his career.

I myself had a run-in with some bad hombres on Portales Road. I left Fort Sumner early one morning to go to our ranch at the Tu-les. About halfway across the sandhills between Stinking Springs and the Tu-les, I came down into a small valley and saw two riders on horseback approaching. I knew there was something wrong when they pulled their neckerchiefs up over their faces and waved to me to leave the road and go around.

"[Pat] Garrett and his posse made headquarters in this warehouse and kept track of visitors to the store by spying on them from the bullet holes in the door."

"This here road's as much mine as it is theirs," I told myself. I didn't move. Then a shot knocked up the sand in front of me. At that I signaled with my left hand, showing that I would circle to the left. I didn't want no trouble with the likes of them, for I had heard that Pat Garrett and a posse from Roswell had started toward Fort Sumner to apprehend a couple of bandits making their way west from Texas.

Pat Garrett had a smooth way of catching men who landed in Fort Sumner to lay in supplies. The only store there was owned and run by J. H. Teets. It was part of the old soldier barracks built in 1864. Teets' store room was thirty feet long, with a post office at the south corner. There was a partition with a door which led into the adjoining warehouse. This old door was marked with several bullet holes. In fact, everything around the place seemed to have been shot up at times. Garrett and his posse made headquarters in this warehouse and kept track of visitors to the store by spying on them from the bullet holes in the door.

I waited on the Portales Road until the bandits had ridden out of sight, then circled and rode straight down the divide between Cibilo Arroyo and Taiban, arriving in Fort Sumner about ten that night. I immediately went to the warehouse and sure enough found Garrett there with his posse. "I will take care of them when they come," he said. "I'll tell Teets to place them in a position along the counter so that I can see them from my peephole in the door."

Next morning early the bandits rode up to the store, went in, and asked for some canned goods and crackers. The merchant kept them occupied with questions until he was sure that Garrett had heard them and knew who they were.

With drawn guns Garrett and his men opened the door, leaped to within a few feet of their backs, and shouted, "You're covered, throw them guns down on the floor!" They gave up without a shot being fired, were handcuffed, and within a few minutes were being escorted to jail.

All kinds of men, good and bad, sooner or later went down the old Portales Road. It has seen lots of history in the making, but never again will times be as rough as they were when the plains were unsettled and cattle trailed through on the long road to market.

TWELVE

EARLY-DAY SALOONS

Nothing cuts the alkali trail dust from a cowpuncher's throat any neater than a good slug of straight whiskey. The thought of "bellyin' up to the bar" when the herd was delivered kept many a rider in his saddle day after monotonous day. I knew all the saloons and bartenders along the many trails I traveled. One reason for this was the fact that a saloon offered quick shelter from any kind of weather, summer heat or winter cold, for often us boys had no other place to go when we hit a new town. Just as often, that's where we wanted to go anyway.

I best knew the famous old Beaver Smith Saloon that the flooding Pecos washed away at Fort Sumner. Farther south there was Kline's Road House on the Hondo River and another on the Fort Stanton–Las Vegas road known as Greathouse's Place. The Spence brothers ran a saloon at Pinos Wells, and Bob Ford, the slayer of Jesse James, kept a bar at Las Vegas.

In contrast to these rough early-day whiskey-pourers, the saloons around Clayton were run by some of the communities' best citizens. Bartending was a respectable business that reaped quick profits from cowboys just ending a long drive.

Some of these profits were put to good use by an enterprising preacher known as Pa Thompson. He was soliciting funds to build a church and on a trade-out with saloon keepers, persuaded them to contribute money as freely as their whiskey flowed. The necessary funds were quickly raised and Pa Thompson let up a heap on his fiery sermons on the evils of liquor.

I was in Charley Meredith's place, when I was introduced to a feller just in from the Sacramento Mountains named Andy McDonald. He was a grizzled old trail boss who shook hands with the comment, "I used to be a deacon in your Pa's church at Uvalde, Texas."

I gave him a quick answer: "Well, Mac, I'm surprised to see a deacon in a place like this."

His come-back sure put me in my place. "I'm shocked to see my preacher's son taking 'em straight over the bar," he replied.

But I wasn't ashamed to be seen in Charley's place by a deacon or anybody else. Meredith was the squarest man I ever dealt with. His poker room served as an office for many a big deal, buying and selling of cattle. Charley would not allow an itinerant rounder to hang around his place at all. Men piking* at his tables were sure that no one dealt Charley's cards except real square dealers.

Upright men like Meredith and others kept Clayton from having the biggest boot hill in the west.

---

*From piker, a stingy person who bets with money not his own.

THIRTEEN

THE OLD BUNK HOUSE

In the early settlement of the west, as a cattle trader, I visited most of the early-day ranches. Sometimes I would be given the only spare room on the place and other times I would be sent to the bunkhouse with the rest of the cowboys. Sometimes I would not be very welcome, and it was hard to get some old puncher to divide bedding with me in cold weather. Finally I studied up a scheme that worked fine for several months. When I was undressing in the bunkhouse, I would casually tell the boys that I was subject to fits during the night. Sometimes I would snap my teeth together and throw my head around just to liven up my story. This resulted in my bunking companion leaving me to throw in with another feller. In most cases, after such a scare, they would give me a good share of the bedding just to keep me in a bed to myself.

Once when I was out contracting cattle to be delivered to the New England Livestock ranch at Fort Sumner, I managed to have a special space all to myself by starting to throw one of them fits. The next night I arrived at another ranch just before bedtime and the owner lit a lantern to show me where the bunkhouse was located. This one looked much better than the dugout I had slept in the night before. It had a plank floor with one large bed, clean sheets, and two pillows, besides plenty of space on the

*". . . I decided to scare him out of the big bed onto the floor.
I told him how I chewed on the feller . . . the night before during
one of my fits."*

floor for extra bedrolls. Sam Smith said to me, "Jack, you can have the big bed. You will be somewhat disturbed before morning when my hands who are out to a dance come in. There's a feller still here who will occupy the room with you as he had to stay behind to help me with the chores. Make yourself to home, now. I'll feed your horse."

Well, the old boy who had stayed to do the work was watching me undress, and I decided to scare him out of the big bed onto the floor. I told him how I had chewed on the feller who had slept with me the night before during one of my fits. He believed every word of my yarn and wouldn't turn out the light but kept eyeing me, real peculiar like. When he thought I was asleep, he went outside and brought in a stick of firewood which he laid beside him on the floor.

When the first bunch came back home from the dance, one of them asked, "Who's that hombre in the big bed by himself?" My companion answered in a low voice. "Shhh, he's a fitty old devil who lives down on the Pecos at Fort Sumner. He told me when he had a fit last night he chewed up his bed feller pretty bad."

That night I surely had a good sleep as no one came near the big bed to disturb me. Next morning when the rising bell rang and all of us began to dress, I decided to pull off another stunt, which really was uncalled for. I thought it would be fun to give the boys just a little scare for good measure so I commenced snapping my teeth, grabbed a pillow, held it in my mouth, and shook it violently. Suddenly the old boy standing next to me busted me over the head with that piece of stove wood. When I came to myself, I was bound, hand and feet, with a rope and about three or four of the boys sitting a-straddle me. One was at my head giving me a few extra licks and another had gagged me to keep me from hollerin'.

My host heard the racket coming from the bunkhouse and opened the door to investigate. "What the Sam Hill is the matter in here?" he demanded.

One of them answered, "This old devil is sure fitty, and we are just curing him of that ugly habit of his."

Of course I felt somewhat humiliated when they finally let me up, but the humiliation wasn't as bad as having my scheme to get a bed to myself laid wide open and exposed.

FOURTEEN

A DELAYED
CHRISTMAS

When the fall roundups were finished and the remudas had been sent off to the winter range, cowboys flocked into old Fort Sumner to attend Mexican bailes and other festivities. The women were busy getting up early Christmas orders from eastern mail houses, for packages had to be shipped back by express to Las Vegas, at least 125 miles away. In the meantime the cowboys chipped in about a hundred dollars to buy some "refreshments" for the Christmas holidays. Then the problem arose as to who to send to Las Vegas to bring back the orders and refreshments.

It happened that Barney Mason had bought four condemned horses and a secondhand wagon to start a freight line to Las Vegas, but his honesty in regard to handling the valuable part of the Christmas cargo, the *wet* part, was seriously questioned. However, he won the contract any way, and on December 15 pulled out of town, his pockets jingling with money.

Preparations for the celebration were on everyone's mind. Invitations were sent to all the neighboring ranchmen for the festivities which were to include a Christmas tree and a grand baile to be pulled off on Christmas Eve. As the time neared, people poured into Fort Sumner from all the surrounding communities.

But Barney and his valuable cargo were nowhere in sight and there had been no word from him. When it finally became evident that Barney had failed us, one of the boys went over to Teet's Store and bought up all the candy in stock. "We've got to entertain them women and children somehow or they'll sure be a disappointed bunch," he explained. Well, we had a celebration of sorts, and the people went on back home, forgetting about their orders and gifts.

Long about February a poor, skinny team of horses with a rickety wagon drew up in front of Barney Mason's house on the outskirts of town. A posse of cowboys was not long in forming to pay him a call with Hugh Leeper, the Sanctified Texan, as spokesman. When Barney responded to their shout to come out, he hit the front steps a'smilin' and a'talkin'. He explained, "Boys, I'm satisfied that when you hear my story you will not be so sore at me."

Leeper was pretty short with him. "What did you do with the *wet* part of our Christmas cargo. Do you have any of it left?"

"Now don't get too hasty," Barney replied. "You see, it was thisaway. I arrived at Las Vegas, stone sober, loaded up my Christmas orders, and pulled out, still as sober as I am now. While passing through Romeroville, I happened to think of an old amigo down at Anton Chico, not much out of my way. I paid him a visit. We went over to the Chameleon Saloon where a lively monte game was running. Well, I commenced piking my expense wad, and my luck began to soar. Inside of an hour I had broke the monte bank. In another hour I had won the saloon, stock and fixtures, and had taken possession with the key safe in my pocket. I was now the owner of a fine business and a cargo of valuable Christmas goods.

I thought it my duty to stay and run my business a while and deliver the freight later. Trade was good during the holidays and I borrowed from your Christmas *wet* order until I could replace it. A few days later two gamblers came down from Santa Fe and asked me to deal them up a lay. They bet the entire size of my bankroll and won. I kept putting up collateral to replenish my bank until they had won my entire business, also teams and wagon.

"My key had to be turned over to them, and they kindly advanced me fifty cents to pay for my own breakfast. Then I had to borrow one of my teams back to deliver my valuable freight to Fort Sumner. I'm glad to say that the Christmas orders are in good shape, and since I have told you about the disposal of the wet part, I hope my explanation is satisfactory."

There was a long pause after Barney had told his story; then Old Jasper said, "Boys, I'm so mad I could bite a ten-penny nail in two, but there is going to be a Christmas tree celebration right here tomorrow night. You boys saddle up right now and go ever' which way to notify the folks."

Hugh Leeper was selected to be the Santa Claus on account of his preaching gave him a good voice. Someone brought a feather pillow to stuff in his breeches to fill him out since he was so lean, but he wouldn't have none of that foolishness. "I'm not about to be a puddin' belly Santa Claus," he declared.

Then Santa took charge of the decorating. He decided we should have a strictly native, ranch type tree and Christmas party. He sent two Mexicans out to cut sod squares with a nice coat of grass on them. Then we planted a cactus, a sage brush, and a mesquite branch at the entrance of the hall where the party was to be held. Between the sod squares, sand was spread to represent a beat-out trail, the Goodnight–Loving, which came by Fort Sumner. And to make it more real like, a cowboy grave was mounded up with a sign, killed by Indians. Then we laid down some bleached bones and a buffalo head. When it was all done, Santa Hugh gave it the once-over and said, "You boys are some decorators. Now we should do a little something to the tree." He got the presents from Barney's wagon and placed all the mail order packages around the base. Next he ordered two chuck wagons to pull up and start sourdough and fixings for at least a hundred people. Last he declared that good strong coffee would be the only *wet* kind of refreshments that would be served.

That evening when the crowd was all there, Santa Hugh ordered a bunch of the boys to escort him and his pack burros into town on the run. As Santa came round the corner of the parade-ground fence, the fellers cut loose with their pistols, and it was a noisy, smoky, powder-scented reception that they gave him. At the hall, Santa made a speech telling why he had been delayed in reaching the bunch at Fort Sumner. He said, "While crossing the Sangre de Cristo mountains in deep snow, my reindeer gave plumb out. I took them to the foothills to graze and rest, and while I was asleep, they strayed off, leaving me afoot. The only thing I could do was to go to a Mexican ranch and buy me some burros to carry my Christmas cargo to Fort Sumner. So here I am at last, wishing everyone a Merry, Merry Christmas." At the end of his speech Santa shook hands with all the children and told their mothers to come up and find their Christmas orders at the base of the tree.

Old Broncho Pete started up a song and shouted, "There's goin' to be a dance at the Old Fort tonight. Join in everbody!"

Caller, let no echo slumber
Fiddler sweatin' like a steer,

Hoof a-poundin' at the lumber,
Making music stars can hear.

Hug the Gals up when you swing 'em;
Raise them plumb off'n their feet.
Balance all, you saddle warmers,
Rag a little, skate your feet.

On to the next 'un and retreat;
Balance to the next in waitin'
Promenade and off you go,
Seat your partners and let 'em blow!"

And where was the feller that said we could not have a big celebration and dance, with only black coffee for refreshment? As I can remember it, our delayed Christmas went down in Fort history as the best we ever had.

FIFTEEN

THE BATTLE OF ESTANCIA GRANT

Frequently in the early 1880s the title to land beyond the Pecos River was in dispute. Since obtaining a court decision as to the legal ownership of land was usually a long and costly affair, many of these disputes were settled on the spot and often with bloodshed. That was the way the dispute at Estancia was settled—with bloodshed.

A bunch of California capitalists acquired title to the Estancia Grant, a strip of valley land about thirty miles long and four or five miles wide which was incorporated under the laws of the Territory as the New Mexico Land and Cattle Company. Having acquired this land, they made plans to stock the range with ten thousand head of cattle and adopted a double circle(0 0) brand, which also was the name of the ranch.

Joel B. Whitney was appointed general manager to stock the range, as both Whitney and the men he represented thought the title to the land was clear. At that time there were only a few settlers on the premises, mostly transient sheep men who followed grass and available watering places. Jim Stinson began to bring in the first four herds of stock cattle.

One of Whitney's first acts when he arrived on the scene was to order all of the settlers off the land. Two of these men were M. B. Otero and a Dr. Henriquez, who claimed a valid title to the old Estancia Ranch, about two thousand acres included in the original grant. Otero was not on the property when Whitney took over, but it is quite probable that when news came to him that the grant had been acquired by California interests and that his title was in danger, he went immediately to investigate.

Whitney and his men were in the ranch house when Otero and two cowboys reined up and dismounted. Otero stepped to the front door, opened it, and demanded that Whitney explain his presence there. Whitney, who was seated at a table covered with papers and ledger books, with his gun beside them, answered with the threatening words as he cocked the pistol, "I'm here by *this* authority." So many guns spoke at once that no one could say afterward who fired the first shot.

In the melee Otero was killed, another man not identified until later also died, and two more were seriously wounded. Whitney himself received two slugs in his body and another in the jaw. The ranch house was such a bloody mess that it was not fit for human habitation.

Whitney's men put him in a spring wagon and drove to Chilili, where two strong horses replaced the ponies first hitched up. He made a painful trip to Albuquerque to be loaded on a train to San Francisco where he made a slow recovery. His facial contour was never the same and he spoke with difficulty.

Metcalf replaced Whitney as manager. He took a more reasonable attitude, persuading his company that it would be wiser to move their headquarters up the arroyo to La Berenda springs. By the time Jim Stinson arrived with his cattle, the situation had quieted down considerably but flared anew when the Parker County cowboys who rode with the herd began to shoot up the town at any excuse. The cowboys were wilder than the Texas range cattle they had herded. Everyone of these men had a "record" of law violation, and it seemed that there was no repentance in any of them. John Green, the Wright brothers, John Jackson (called Happy), Oscar Armstrong (the Rooster), Arkansas Sandy, Steve Bootherby, Green Davis, Bill Lee, and Jim Stroud were as tough a lot as ever prodded a cow down the trail.

Stinson himself was unable to cope with these codgers, and the new manager Metcalf had no better luck. Whenever the Mexicans at the Otero Ranch celebrated fiesta, the cowboys from the Double Circle arrived to take part by stirring up trouble that ended in fist fights, knifings, and occasional gunplay. Bill Lee was justifiably shot by a Mexican whom he had "playfully" roped while the man was crossing the plaza. Two more boys were killed at Paint Horse Mesa, with innumerable quarrels constantly stirring up strife. To keep peace with the neighboring ranchers, Metcalf finally fired the whole bunch at the end of the roundup in 1887.

At least he tried to let all of them go, but there was one cowboy who wouldn't be fired. When Metcalf gave him his notice with his final check, Happy Jack replied, "You can pay me off and take my mount, but you can't force me to leave this place. I'm part of the fixtures around here and I aim to stay. Sabe?" And stay he did, becoming roundup boss as long as a cow grazed their range.

In 1890 the title to the Estancia Grant was annuled in Federal Court, forcing the New Mexico Land and Cattle Company to close out. The land they claimed was surveyed and opened to homesteaders. The Double Circle Ranch was closed, but the Otero Ranch was not, as M. B. Otero's title held good. His daughter, Mrs. Otero Warren, reported later that the final tract of land in the old Estancia Ranch was sold in 1902 to the New Mexico Central Railroad because of its valuable water supply.

SIXTEEN

NEGRO COWBOYS

I believe the most noted Negro cowboy on the northern range was George McJunkin who came over the Goodnight Trail with a colony of Texas pioneers with Gid Roberds family and, believe me, they raised him right. In his fifty years on the range as a cowhand, he never was known to cause any trouble, and every cowboy around would try to protect him if some stranger got smart-alecky.

On the roundups when the cook notified the boys to "come get it" most every one would make a run for the plate pile. But not George. He just stood until the last tenderfoot kid or Mexican hand, even the horse wrangler, had served himself, and then he would come up to help his plate from the cook pot.

Good-natured and smiling, laughing at jokes, he would make remarks about his own color and background. I remember a roundup in 1894 when Negro George was present, representing the Crow Foot outfit. Buck Miller was in charge of the wagon and planned a trip into Folsom. He asked the boys standing around the wagon if he could bring them anything from town. George spoke up right quick like with a broad grin on his face. "Yassir, Boss, you jest bring me some complexion powders!"

Negro George worked the last thirty years of his life for W. H. Jack, manager of the Crow Foot Cattle Co. Mr. Jack had large interests in the south part of the state and turned overseeing the Crow Foot Ranch to George who matured the young stock for shipment. He did his work very well, was a valuable asset to his company, and never had an enemy that I knew of. He discovered an important archeological site near Folsom in 1911.

*   *   *

Negro Add drifted up from the Guadalupe bottoms of south Texas to the high plains of New Mexico, where he worked for Major G. W. Littlefield for the rest of his life. He was a familiar figure at every roundup, for when the horses were fresh, he "sapped out the salty ones" that the boys hated to ride. It was nothing unusual for him to top-off several horses in the morning to get the pitching out of their systems before the outfit started on the move. I have seen him kick the living daylights out of jug-head horses that wouldn't stop pitching. He rode as if born in the saddle, raked the spurs across hair and hide when a horse "swallowed his head." So far as I know, he was thrown only once and then by a horse they called Whistling Bullet because he whistled through his nose.

When Roswell was just a cowtown, Old Add was sitting on a Bar F roping horse in front of the only hotel when a driverless team of horses hitched to a milk wagon came clattering down the street at a fast clip. He always kept his rope tied hard and fast to the saddle horn, so when the team came near enough, he built a long loop, ran along side of them and caught them both around their necks, real clean like. Then he pitched the slack over the wagon, dropped it over his left stirrup and turned off, upsetting the whole works in the middle of the street. The wagon was wrecked, the milk poured from broken bottles, and the horses bruised up a bit. When the driver caught up with his runaway team and removed Add's rope from around their necks, he was flabbergasted at the Negro's comment, "Them horses sure would of torn things up if I hadn't caught 'em!"

Add was not polite like George McJunkin at the chuck wagon. He would come crawling up on all fours, push into the waiting line, and fill his plate right after the top hands. No one challenged him, perhaps because he was so strong. Also he had the reputation of never fighting. Perhaps this kept him out of trouble so it added years to his life.

There was never a Littlefield trail too long for him to ride. He rode until he was so crippled with rheumatism that he could not mount his horse alone. Then one day, like a man who knew his time had come, he just lay down on his bed and died.

*   *   *

Old Frank was a Chisum slave who refused to take his freedom. He remained with the Chisum family all his life. He was real black, lean, ugly, and stuttered, but like John Chisum, he was chock full of wisdom and plain horse sense. Many times a competitor would try to pump him for information about his boss, but when old Frank began to stutter and make faces trying to get his words out, they would give up and go about their business. Yes, old Frank was smart and loyal as they come.

He knew more about Chisum's ranch than most any relative that Chisum had, and was trusted to inspect the range and cattle and come back with a truthful report. When John Chisum died, the estate was mismanaged and the Chisum relatives turned their cattle into the Jingle-Bob Cattle Co. Frank refused to go along as he wanted to keep his herd and own brand to himself. "I want to see that VF brand and know exactly which are my cows [he said]. I want to see that VF brand and know that the animal belongs to me alone, not to a company."

And Frank was plumb right about this. Later when the manager and all the Chisums went broke, Frank still had his little herd. Old Frank who had watched Sally Chisum, the Queen of the Jingle-Bobs, grow up, came to her rescue when she was ordered to vacate the home and ranch. He then sold his herd, bought her a new ranch, and stocked it with sheep. Though it was small, with his good management, they made a go of it.

Frank lived in Roswell after he retired. He usually led the rodeo parades on horseback, carrying the flag. He always wished that John Chisum was riding beside him, although he outlived his master by twenty years. He went back to Paris, Texas shortly before his death and was buried close beside Chisum's grave. He was as devoted in death as he had been all his life.

*   *   *

Another Negro cowhand that I recall was Negro Bill, a Schreiner Negro, who had come to the Pecos River region in 1884 with a herd from Texas. He worked ten years for the Fort Sumner Land and Cattle Co. with Dan Taylor, the owner. He was dependable, intelligent, well-mannered, and knew the cow business as well as his boss. His unfortunate death came at the hands of a Mexican on Taylor's ranch in Picket Wire Canyon, Colorado.

*   *   *

Bose Ikard was Charles Goodnight's trusty hand. When the Colonel drove over that terrible Horse Head crossing and the difficult Pecos River route, the Graveyard of Hopes it was called, Bose was right there to keep the herd pointed north. In those early days, after making a summer drive a thousand miles to Pueblo, Colorado, cowboys had to back-trail with a pack horse to carry bedding and supplies. There was no "riding the cushions"

135

back like the later hands did after the railroads came in. Old Bose was not like the other cowboys who would blow a few dollars on a nifty outfit to wear around the saloons and monte parlors. He just kept his same old rags. Once when Goodnight had sold a herd at Pueblo, he rigged up a pack outfit to take $25,000 over the trail he had blazed. He usually carried his money in a belt buckled around his waist, but this time, because he was afraid of bandits along the way, he made old Bose wear the money belt. He knew Bose looked so much like a tramp that no one would search him for any cash.

When Goodnight finally quit the trail to settle at his Palo Duro ranch, he and Bose, though still friends, parted company. Bose did not mind making cattle drives, but he did not want to leave his own people permanently. When Goodnight received the message that faithful Bose had passed on to his reward, he erected a tombstone over his grave with the inscription: "Bose Ikard, a good citizen, dependable, honest, and my trusted body guard for many years."

*　　*　　*

The Panhandle of Texas now has the most famous cowhand still living, Matthew Bones (Negro Bones). He has mingled with cowmen, working cattle, breaking broncs for a half century, and now is a wealthy realtor who rides herd over a colony of over three thousand Negros in North Heights, Amarillo, Texas. These people are all law-abiding and honest. Bones' weapon is the old wet rope treatment for those who get out of hand, so he has no trouble in making them all behave themselves!

*　　*　　*

Every ranch and every trail drive had colored hands who worked hard, rode hard, and were generally respected by all. Of course, as in any part of society, white or black, some were better than others, but for the most part, they were trusted friends.

SEVENTEEN

DEATH AND BURIAL OF BILLY THE KID

Coroner's Verdict
Territory of New Mexico
Precinct No. 27
County of San Miguel

To the attorney of the First Judicial District of the Territory of New Mexico: GREETINGS:

This, the fifteenth of July, A.D. 1881, I, the undersigned Justice of the Peace of the precinct above named, received information that there has been a death in Fort Sumner in said precinct, and immediately upon receiving information, proceeded to the said place and named M. Rudolph, Jose Silva, Antonio Savedra, Pedro Antonio Lucero, Lorenzo Jaramillo, and Sabel Guitierrez as a jury to investigate the matter and the meeting in the house of Lucien B. Maxwell. The said jury proceeded to a room in said house where they found the body of William Bonney, alias "Billy the Kid" with a bullet wound in his chest on the left side, and having examined the body, they examined the evidence of Pedro Maxwell which is as follows:

While Pat Garrett was sitting on the corner of my bed talking to me, Billy the Kid came to the door with pistol in hand and asked me, 'Quien es (Who is it?) Quienes son los hombres afuera? (Who are the men outside?) And when Pat Garrett fired two shots at him the said William Bonney fell on one side of my fireplace. Then I left the room. When I returned several minutes later the said Bonney was dead.

The jury has found the following verdict: We of the jury unanimously find that William Bonney was killed by a shot in his left breast in the region of the heart, fired from a pistol in the hands of Pat Garrett. And our verdict is that the act of said Garrett was justifiable homicide. And we are unanimous in the opinion that the gratitude of the whole community is due to said Garrett for the act, and that he deserves to be rewarded.

M. Rudolph, President
Antonio Savedra
Pedro Antonio Lucero
Jose Silva
Sabel Guitierrez
Lorenzo Jaramillo

> Alejandro Seguro, Justice
> of Peace, San Miguel Co.*

This is the way Jack Potter told the exciting story of the Kid:

Billy had been dead three years when I came to Fort Sumner in 1884, but folks there were still talking about him and the way Garrett shot him in the dark. The people of the Fort, home of Billy's staunch friends and his ladylove as well, were awakened just past midnight as news of the killing spread by excited messengers to each adobe dwelling. There was much wailing and weeping among the women: "El pobre Beely, pobre Beely (poor Billy)." Both factions of the male citizens, those who mourned his passing and those who agreed that Garrett should be rewarded, were excited and confused over the death.

The Sheriff instructed several Mexican ranch hands to remove the dirt roof of an abandoned adobe building and pull out enough ceiling planks to make a coffin, as time was too short to have new lumber shipped from Las Vegas.

Late in the afternoon, the corpse was loaded into Old Vicente's wood-hauling wagon which proceeded to the government cemetery followed by every person in Fort Sumner, even the saloon keeper who rarely closed down his business. The Sanctified Texan, who believed in predestination, preached the funeral and said that Billy's time had certainly come at last.

---

*This document appears in Poe, John W., *The Death of Billy the Kid*, Houghton Mifflin, Boston and New York, 1933, pp. 56-58.

They told me he made remarks about Billy, "our beloved young citizen," and read from the 14th chapter of Job—"A man that is born of woman is of few days and is full of trouble—he fleeth like a shadow and continueth not." In closing he said, "Billy cannot come back to us, but we can go to him and will see him again up yonder, Amen."

The day after the funeral Pete Maxwell had his man pull a wooden picket from the parade-ground fence, saw off a foot or so, and nail it in a crossbar to the longer piece. Then he printed in crude letters "BILLY THE KID, JULY 14, 1881."

Later this marker was stolen by relic seekers and the second one, which replaced it, was also stolen. Now a granite stone marks the lonely grave, but it too has been chipped and scratched. Back in 1930 when I began to write down my memories, I had a letter from John Roark, a stagecoach driver, who swore he saw the uprooted grave marker strapped to a feller's luggage as he boarded a train back East.

I was riding along with Pete Maxwell and I asked him how he felt when he realized that he was trapped in bed between Sheriff Garrett and Billy the Kid. He drew up his reins, thought a minute and said: "I wish you had not asked me that question as I have tried to forget it all. I realized that I had three chances at being killed on the spot in the next instant. First by being between the two men; next, when the Kid fell forward, the butcher knife he had used to cut meat plunged close to my chest; and last, as I got out of bed to escape, I was stopped at the door by Deputy John Poe with his .45 in my stomach. The Deputy thought I was the Kid. I had a lot of explaining to do, pronto!"

So this was the final chapter in the life of one of the most colorful characters of the entire West. Billy was what you might call a gentleman desperado and a large number of people counted him a friend. As time goes on, future readers of Billy the Kid history will wonder whether the stories are true or just plain fiction. But to some of us old timers who lived through those days, *Billicito* still rides the country around and beyond the Pecos.

EIGHTEEN

COWBOY AND
SHEEP GOVERNORS

I t is always interesting to come to Santa Fe, and it occurs to me
that it would be timely to write about the Governor's Mansion under
different administrations. When New Mexico became a state in 1912 and
McDonald was elected its first governor, the cowmen went wild with joy.
While Bill McDonald was never what you would call an old Waddie, nevertheless he did handle large cattle interests and was generally considered as
a cowman. When he moved into the Governor's Mansion, he tried to make
it look as near as possible like the Bar W Ranch.

When McDonald's term expired, we had mostly lawyers who were
governor until the fall of 1922. Then news spread like a dust storm on the
prairie that Jim Hinkle, a dyed-in-the-hide cow-puncher, had been nominated on the Democratic ticket for governor. Then on election day, cowboys came in from every isolated cow camp in New Mexico. James Hinkle
was elected in a walkaway.

I was with the first bunch of cowmen to visit him after he moved into
the mansion, and found that he had lost no time in shaping it up like the C
A Bar Ranch. There were horses hobbled out around roundup beds spread
on the lawn; old slickers and saddles straddled the iron fence; a big beef
hung up on the shady side, and best of all, a long string of jerked meat was
tied up with a rope against the wall.

Governor Hinkle hung out at the De Vargas Hotel as much as he did at the Capitol, telling stories not only to his old time friends, but to plenty of tenderfoot legislators and easterners. 1923 and '24 were two big years for us cowmen, and then came Hannett, a lawyer governor who was a fine gentleman but a stranger to the saddle. A different crowd congregated around the mansion, mostly lawyer folk and white-collary visitors. It was a sad day for us cowmen when *Borreguero* (Sheepman) Dick Dillon beat Governor Hannett in the election of 1926. This meant that the mansion which had been shaped up before as a headquarters ranch house, would soon be changed into a sheep camp. And in a short while, dozens of *borreguerros, pastores* (shepherds), and *trasquiladores* (sheepshearers) came to visit the *gran capitán de los borregueros* (grand captain of the sheepmen).

There were dozens of pack burros grazing in the nearby Santa Fe River and on the lawn of the mansion. Several muttons hung on the shady side where beef had formerly been strung. *Cocineros* (cooks) rolled out *bunvuelo* (bun) dough to the tune of *guitarras*. This was such a humiliation to the cowpunchers in the legislature that they would turn their heads and shut their eyes when they passed the mansion.

In the fall of 1929, Robert Dow, a knight of the saddle, had a Don Quixote idea that he was the hombre to capture the governship from the Borreguero Dillon and turn the mansion back to the hands of a true cattle-man of the Democratic Party. Dow was one of those roping and riding kind of cowmen, the rodeo class. When he campaigned, he hooked a trailer behind his car to take his roping horse to give exhibitions while he asked for votes. Dow had dreams of roping his way into the governor's office. At the mansion he planned to erect riding shutes and a fenced-in track for bulldogging and steer roping. But his plans went astray, for Richard Dillon kept his sheep camp there two years longer. Finally the mansion was turned over to Arthur Seligman, a banker, and things were never the same again.

NOTES

THE LIFE OF COL. JACK POTTER

1 Fightin' Parson's Boy

[1] The biography of Andrew Jackson Potter, prepared as a Master's thesis titled "Texas History" by Mary L. Fitzgerald, Midwestern University, Wichita Falls, Texas, 1968–69, served as source material for this chapter. Facts of Jack Potter's early years were noted in biographical data in the Potter Files given by family members to Special Collections, Eastern New Mexico University Library, Portales, New Mexico.

2 Trailing Up from Texas

[1] Jack Potter, *Cattle Trails of the Old West*, p. 16.
[2] Garnet M. and Herbert O. Brayer, *American Cattle Trails, 1540–1900*, p. 25.
[3] *Ibid.*, p. 28.
[4] Potter, *Cattle Trails*, p. 10.
[5] Brayer, *American Cattle Trails*, p. 51.
[6] *Ibid.*, p. 62.
[7] Jack Potter, *Union County Leader*, Clayton, New Mexico, undated clipping in the Potter Files. All clippings from the *Union County Leader* referred to in the notes are located in the Potter Files, Special Collections, Eastern New Mexico University Library, Portales, New Mexico.

[8] Marguerite Riordan, "Col. Jack Potter, Last of the Old Time Trail Drivers," p. 27.

[9] Frank King, *Longhorn Trail Drivers*, p. 47.

[10] *Ibid.*, p. 114.

[11] Harry S. Drago, *Great American Cattle Trails*, p. 240.

[12] J. Marvin Hunter, *Trail Drivers of Texas*, pp. 62–70.

[13] Jack Potter, "The Cowboy Metropolis," *Union County Leader*, undated clipping in Potter Files.

[14] *Ibid.*

[15] J. Evetts Haley, "Texas Fever and Winchester Quarantine," pp. 38–41.

3 On the Trail to Romance

[1] Jack Potter, *Lead Steers*, pp. 17–20.

[2] Ethel Potter Wade, interview conducted by Jean M. Burroughs, Clayton, New Mexico, October 17, 1975, housed in Special Collections, Eastern New Mexico University Library, Portales, New Mexico.

[3] S. Omar Barker, "Jack Potter's Courtin'," *Ranch Romances*, September 1941. Also printed in *Rawhide Rhymes*, Doubleday and Co., New York, n.d. Quoted with the kind permission of the author.

4 The Fort Sumner Years

[1] Territorial Records of Incorporation, State Records Center and Archives, Santa Fe.

[2] *Ibid.*

[3] *Ibid.*

[4] Carl Hatch, U.S. Senator, to Jack Potter, Potter Files.

[5] Jack Potter, "Old Fort Sumner," n.p., Potter Files.

[6] King, *Longhorn Trail Drivers*, p. 71.

[7] Jack Potter, "Tragedies on the National Cattle Trail," *Union County Leader*, undated clipping in Potter Files.

[8] Brayer, *American Cattle Trails*, p. 80.

[9] *Ibid.*

[10] Jack Potter, *Union County Leader*, undated clipping in Potter Files.

[11] Ira G. Clark, *Then Came the Railroads*, p. 105.

5 From the Pecos to the Dry Cimarron

[1] Elvis E. Fleming, "The Texas–New Mexico Boundary," *Southwest Heritage* 5, no. 1: 38.

[2] Mary Robinson, "The Question of the 103rd Meridian," *Roosevelt County: History and Heritage*, ed. J. Burroughs (Portales, New Mexico, 1975), p. 184.

[3] *Ibid.*, p. 185.

[4] Jack Potter, "Tragedies of the Two Mile Strip," *Union County Leader*, February 15, 1945.

[5] *Ibid.*

[6] Jack Potter, "Early Day History of Kenton, Oklahoma," *Union County Leader*, undated clipping in Potter Files.

[7] Jack Potter, *Union County Leader*, undated clipping in Potter Files.

[8] Ethel Potter Wade, interview.

[9] *Ibid.*

[10] Alfred H. Phillips, undated written account, Potter Files, edited by Jean M. Burroughs.

[11] Ethel Potter Wade interview.
[12] *Ibid.*
[13] *Ibid.*
[14] Jack Potter, *Union County Leader*, undated clipping in Potter Files.
[15] Potter, "Early Day History of Kenton."
[16] Jack Potter, "Pioneering in the Cimarron Valley," *Union County Leader*, undated clipping in Potter Files edited by Jean M. Burroughs.

6 Clayton's Colorful Citizen

[1] D. H. Haley, interview conducted by Jean M. Burroughs, Portales, New Mexico, November 7, 1975, housed in Special Collections, Eastern New Mexico University Library, Portales, New Mexico.
[2] Jack Potter, "The Singing Cowboy," *Union County Leader*, undated clipping in Potter Files.
[3] Jack Potter, "Knowing Your Men," *Union County Leader*, undated clipping in Potter Files.
[4] *Ibid.*
[5] *Ibid.*
[6] Jack Potter, *Union County Leader*, undated clipping in Potter Files.
[7] Jack Potter, "The Late Spencer Graves," *Union County Leader*, undated clipping in Potter Files.
[8] Ethel Potter Wade, interview.
[9] Jack Potter, undated clipping in Potter Files.
[10] *Ibid.*
[11] Obituary for Jack Potter, *Union County Leader*, November 29, 1950, named this organization as Trail Drivers and Pioneer Association of New Mexico.

7 Cowboy Author and his Friends

[1] Hunter, *Trail Drivers of Texas*, n.p.
[2] Note, Potter Files.
[3] Excerpt from letter in files of the Nita Stewart Haley Memorial Library, Midland, Texas.
[4] Letter in files of the Nita Stewart Haley Memorial Library.
[5] Letter in files of the Nita Stewart Haley Memorial Library.
[6] Letter in files of the Nita Stewart Haley Memorial Library.
[7] Jack Potter, "Pioneering on the Leader Staff—A Review," Part 1, *Union County Leader*, undated clipping in Potter Files.
[8] *Ibid.*
[9] *Ibid.*
[10] *Ibid.*
[11] Jack Potter, "Pioneering on the Leader Staff—A Review," Part 2, *Union County Leader*, undated clipping in Potter Files.
[12] *Ibid.*
[13] Letter in files of the Nita Stewart Haley Memorial Library.
[14] Letter in files of the Nita Stewart Haley Memorial Library.
[15] Letter in files of the Nita Stewart Haley Memorial Library.
[16] Letter in files of the Nita Stewart Haley Memorial Library.
[17] *Ibid.* The reference to "Fanny" is to the editor of *Ranch Romances*, Fanny Ellsworth.
[18] Jack Potter, *Union County Leader*, undated clipping in Potter Files.
[19] George Fitzpatrick, "Off the Beaten New Mexico Path," *New Mexico Tribune*, March 19, 1934.

[20] Jack Potter, "Capture of Geronimo and His Apaches," *Union County Leader*, 1932.

[21] These titles were confirmed by the present editor of *New Mexico Magazine* in a letter to me dated November 3, 1975.

[22] *New Mexico Magazine*, March 1934.

[23] *New Mexico Magazine*, February 1934.

[24] Undated notes, Potter Files.

[25] Jack Potter, *Union County Leader*, undated clipping in Potter Files.

[26] Letter in files of the Nita Stewart Haley Memorial Library.

[27] Letter, Jack Potter to J. Frank Dobie, Potter Files.

[28] Letter, Jack Potter to J. Frank Dobie, Potter Files.

[29] WPA Writers' Project Files, State Records Center and Archives, Santa Fe.

8 *End of the Trail*

[1] Jack Potter, "The Swede Kid and the Bishop," *Union County Leader*, undated clipping in Potter Files.

[2] WPA Writers' Project Files, State Records Center and Archives.

[3] Cordelia Potter, *Union County Leader*, November 1944.

[4] Obituary for Cordelia Potter, *Union County Leader*, June 1948.

[5] Letter, S. Omar Barker to Jack Potter, used here by kind permission of Mr. Barker.

[6] Letter, Jack Potter to J. Frank Dobie, Potter Files.

[7] Obituary for Jack Potter, *Union County Leader*, November 29, 1950.

BIBLIOGRAPHY

Adams, Brown. *Three Ranches West.* Carlton Press, New York, 1972.

Brayer, Garner M., and Herbert O. *American Cattle Trails, 1540–1900.* Smith Brooks Printing Co., Denver, 1952.

Clark, Ira G. *Then Came the Railroads.* University of Oklahoma Press, Norman, 1958.

Clay, John. *My Life on the Range.* University of Oklahoma Press, Norman, 1962.

Collinson, Frank. *My Life in the Saddle.* Edited by Mary W. Clarke. University of Oklahoma Press, Norman, 1963.

Dale, E. E. *Frontier Trails.* University of Oklahoma Press, Norman, 1966.

Dobie, Frank. *Cow People.* Little, Brown and Co., Boston, 1964.

Drago, Harry S. *Great American Cattle Trails.* Branham House, New York, 1965.

Fergusson, Harvey. *Rio Grande.* Alfred A. Knopf, New York, 1933.

Fitzgerald, Mary L. "Texas History." Master's thesis, Midwestern University, 1968–69.

Haley, J. Evetts. *Charles Goodnight, Cowman and Plainsman.* University of Oklahoma Press, Norman, 1949.

———. *Men of Fiber.* Carl Herzog, El Paso, 1963.

———. "Texas Fever and Winchester Quarantine." *Panhandle Plains Historical Review.* 8:38–41.

Holden, W. C. *Alkali Trails.* Southwest Press, Dallas, 1930.

Hunter, J. Marvin, ed. *The Trail Drivers of Texas,* Cokesbury Press, Nashville, 1925.

King, Frank. *Longhorn Trail Drivers.* Haynes Corp., Los Angeles, 1940.

McCarty, John L. *Maverick Town.* University of Oklahoma Press, Norman, 1968.

McCoy, Joseph G. *Historical Sketches of the Cattle Trails*. Ramsey, Millett and Hudson, Kansas City, 1874.

Potter, Jack. *Cattle Trails of the Old West*. Edited by Laura Krehbiel. Leader Press, Clayton, New Mexico, 1939.

————. *Lead Steers*. Edited by Ethylyn Holt Easterday. Leader Press, Clayton, New Mexico, 1939.

Riordan, Marguerite. "Col. Jack Potter, Last of the Old Time Trail Drivers." *The Cattleman*, August 1950, pp. 27, 74–90.

Skaggs, Jimmy. *Cattle Trailing Industry*. University of Kansas, Manhattan, Kansas, 1973.

Street, Floyd. *Prairie Trails and Cow Towns*. Devin–Adair Co., New York, 1963.

Waters, L. L. *Steel Trails to Santa Fe*. University of Kansas, Lawrence, 1950.